adolescence
a parent's guide

adolescence
a parent's guide

> practical
> solutions

> survival scripts
> & scenarios

TARA EGAN, D.Ed.

**ROCKRIDGE
PRESS**

To Demi, Savannah, and Declan,
my favorite adolescents

Contents

Introduction ix

Chapter One: Late Childhood:
But They're Still So Cute!
(Ages 8-ish to 9-ish) **1**

Chapter Two: Early Adolescence:
Cute with a Side of 'Tude
(Ages 10-ish to 12-ish) **11**

Chapter Three: Middle Adolescence:
Less Cute, More Puberty
(Ages 12-ish to 14-ish) **41**

Chapter Four: Late Adolescence:
The World According to Sex
(Ages 15-ish to 18-ish) **69**

Chapter Five: Emerging Adulthood:
Leaving the Nest . . . Maybe
(Ages 19-ish to 25-ish) **105**

References 123

Resources 124

Index 125

Introduction

adolescence always seems sort of mysterious and unpredictable. Everyone craves information about this time of physical awkwardness and emotional turmoil, especially if you have a child at home who's starting to develop lanky limbs and chortle when they hear a sex joke on TV. Books, articles, TV shows, and blog posts about adolescence created only 10 years ago don't stand the test of time, because each generation of adolescents is highly influenced by current events and societal trends. This generation of kids and teens is actively shaped by technology and social media, and we, as parents, are tasked with raising them in a manner that's complementary.

So why are you here? Maybe your eight-year-old is super opinionated and her teacher said in a laughing-but-not-really-funny way, "I can't imagine what she'll be like as a teenager!" Or your 12-year-old hasn't made eye contact with you in six weeks and his room smells like the bottom of a gerbil cage. Maybe your 16-year-old just screamed, "I don't care if I ever go to college because SATs are so DUMB, Mom," before she slammed her bedroom door. Maybe your 20-year-old quit his job *again* and his beard smells vaguely of weed.

Maybe there's part of you that's worried all the time. About your kid. About your parenting. About whether these tough moments are fleeting and typical, or so troubling that they require attention from a professional (hint: They can be both of these at once).

You are not alone. Nearly all parents of adolescents want to simultaneously freeze time so our kid doesn't grow another inch *and* launch them into space (along with a bag of their dirty laundry). But you'll get through this, if for no other reason than time will pass and they'll get older and replace you with a sketchy roommate.

How do I know that you'll get through this? I have a master's and a doctoral degree in school psychology as well as additional graduate training in counseling children, teens, and families. I've worked as a school psychologist for many years, and I've also taught at the college level. In 2011, I became a solo practitioner and started offering parent coaching and counseling services to parents of children and teens dealing with social, emotional, or behavioral issues. These kids are often disrespectful, aggressive, anxious, sad, or poorly regulated. Their parents and I work as a team to transform them into well-adjusted kids and to create healthy family dynamics.

I also know firsthand what it's like to parent youths who are undergoing the transition from childhood to adulthood. I am the mother and stepmother of six kids, all of whom are preteens, teens, or emerging adults, and this has significantly shaped my perspective.

Over the span of this book, we'll discuss how children progress from the relative stability of late childhood, through the peaks and valleys of adolescence, to the tentative exploration of emerging adulthood. We'll learn about their emotional changes, and how their brains develop along with their bodies. Throughout the book, "Brain Change" sidebars will teach you the latest information about adolescent brain science and how it relates to changes in reasoning, sex drive, impulsivity, risk-taking behavior, and disorganization. We'll also track each stage of social development and place all this information in the context of both the parent's *and* the child's experience.

I'll show you some practical solutions that can help you through the day-to-day challenges while still protecting your relationship with your adolescent. Any recommendations given in this book have been used in real life, in my professional work as well as in my personal life as a parent. I always tell the parents I work with that I don't wish to speak *theoretically* about parenting; I want them to acquire specific techniques that can be applied in the home environment as soon as they leave my office.

Along the way, I'll share a few unique tools I've developed to help you figure out how to handle certain sticky situations. "Say This, Not That!" sections will help steer you away from unproductive language to more emotionally responsive communication. And "Limit or Let Go" boxes will help you determine whether a limit-pushing situation is one where you want to hold firm or where you might want to relax.

People raising teens are asked to walk the line between guiding and protecting kids and allowing them to safely explore, learn from their mistakes, and develop a healthy identity. It's a difficult balancing act, and every now and then it's okay (and normal) to fall. No one is perfect, and we all benefit from advice sometimes.

I also want to recognize that it's *you* who knows your child best. If a recommendation in this book doesn't feel right or doesn't seem to apply to your adolescent, then do a mental eye roll and move on to the next one. This book is meant to be only one of the tools in your toolbox, and your toolbox is going to look different from that of the parent in the house next door.

A Note on Language

Throughout the book, I use the term *parent* to refer to anyone caring for a child, and *your child*, *your teen*, or *your adolescent* to refer to the child that the reader cares for. But my writing is informed by the fact that parents are far from the only people raising and caring for a child. Stepparents, grandparents, aunts, uncles, siblings, cousins, and other caregivers can and do provide love, care, guidance, and support to adolescents. This book and its techniques honor all types of families, and they are meant to be utilized by anyone raising a loved one.

Me: **Our boy is so cute.**

Husband: **He smells a little.**

Chapter One

Late Childhood:
But They're Still So Cute!
(Ages 8-ish to 9-ish)

IF YOU HAVE AN EIGHT- OR NINE-YEAR-OLD AT HOME, it may feel like adolescence is still eons away. Nearly everything about your relationship with your child still looks and feels familiar: They'll snuggle with you on the couch, hug and kiss you unprompted, and tell you 95 percent of the thoughts they have on any given day. Their life feels like an open book that you can peruse at any time. Yet while they look and act like a little kid on most days, they're actually on the cusp of adolescence.

In the years ahead, your child will begin to make the physical, emotional, and social journey toward adolescence. What starts off with the physical onset of puberty and spurts of outsize emotions morphs into a period of dealing with social pressure, experimenting with risk-taking behavior, developing identity, and trying to text at the dinner table. While some days with your adolescent will be filled with laughter and productivity, there will be many days (or weeks!) when communication with them will feel unsatisfying, perplexing, and even frustrating. There are a lot of ups and downs during adolescence, for both parents and teens, and it's essential to accumulate some resources to help you through the tough moments.

So What Exactly *Is* Adolescence?

Adolescence, simply put, is a time of change. Your child is transitioning between childhood and adulthood, and they're about to make a lengthy pit stop at a place filled with uncertainty, inconsistency, and big emotions. While adolescence presents a little differently for everyone, it generally spans the time from when hormones trigger menstruation or ejaculation of live sperm to the late teens, when adolescents physically resemble fully grown adults. However, it should be noted that the prefrontal cortex does not finish developing until the mid 20s, so although your older offspring may have the physical appearance and responsibilities of an adult, they may still not yet have the corresponding reasoning abilities.

Adolescence is triggered by the physical changes of, er, *puberty*. My 12-year-old hates that word, so it's fun to beatbox it in the kitchen when I'm unpacking groceries and dangling a new deodorant stick in front of him, urging him to "just use it, son; it won't hurt." Puberty begins as a series of hormone changes quietly percolating under the surface of your sweet eight-year-old's clear skin. It soon erupts into visible changes like rapid weight gain and a burst of height. Boys acquire more muscle, girls accumulate more fat, and hairs on legs and pubic areas begin to sprout one by one. ("Please don't say the word *pubic*, Mom. It is *so* gross.") Due to factors such as increased muscle mass and enhanced gross motor skills among boys, the athletic skills of boys and girls are no longer evenly matched. Acne becomes a constant lament, and masturbation is a topic that is suddenly both extremely relevant and universally uncomfortable.

There are emotional changes, too. Throughout adolescence, there will be moments that seem sudden and explosive, like that time my daughter cried copiously over the father-daughter relationship in a cleaning product commercial. Sometimes these emotional changes result in your teen clinging to you, allowing you to dry their tears and absorbing reassurance that they're still your baby and "omgiloveyousomuch." Other times, they'll snarl at you when you knock on their bedroom door to tell them that dinner is ready, and you'll wonder how old they have to be before you can stop feeling obligated to feed them every darn day. While annoying and unpredictable, these emotional outbursts serve a purpose for your blossoming teen, so it's nice when you have the words to explain this to them. We'll work on how to address these situations later on in the book.

Socially, adolescents are likely to experience whiplash. They want to fit in and feel the approval of their peers, but they also want to feel unique and individual. Sometimes they feel accepted, appreciated, and attractive. Other times, they think hateful things about themselves, and feel convinced that everyone else hates them, too. And because all their friends are going through this same journey, it can cause them to turn on one another at times. They're all struggling to keep their heads above water in the social ocean, so to speak, so they aren't necessarily able to toss a life jacket to a drowning peer.

Plus, the inundation of social media and the subsequent "fear of missing out" that it creates can wreak havoc on their ability to form and maintain healthy relationships with adults, peers, and romantic interests. Our teens have an entirely different view of dating, sex, and their role in the online world than their parents do. And it's not all bad, even though we hear so much about the scary parts. At some point, we need to move beyond judging it to accepting it—even embracing it.

Finally, cognitive changes are in abundance. These brain changes can be extra confusing for parents, because teens seem to vacillate between extreme shrewdness and a lack of common sense. It can be frustrating to have your child go from telling you 1,473 interesting facts about killer sharks as you drive to the beach to leaving the stovetop on for three hours after they've made themselves a grilled cheese. Their reasoning will improve as they go along, but it will ebb and flow depending on the circumstances.

Unfortunately, society seems to paint adolescence as a time of chronic awfulness. We constantly hear adolescence described with adjectives such as *traumatic*, *disturbing*, and *agonizing*, and we send that message to children from an early age. I recall a time my teen stepson stomped out of the room while my seven-year-old son colored at the kitchen table. My seven-year-old then solemnly said to me, "I think he's being teenagery, Mom. He can't help it." While we all know someone who went through a horrible adolescence that led them down a path of bad choices, addiction, or mental illness, in actuality, only a portion of teens struggle with this sort of darkness. Research suggests that it impacts only 15 to 20 percent of teens. It's common enough that we need to stay tuned in, responsive, and proactive, but not nearly as common as popular culture would have you believe. Adolescence is normal, big emotions are okay, and your parenting will have a big influence on how your child navigates this time in their life. So don't get sucked into the hype, parents. It's all going to be okay. I mean, probably not fun. And probably pretty gray-hair inducing. But okay.

Stages of Adolescence

Adolescence is divided into four stages: early adolescence, middle adolescence, late adolescence, and emerging adulthood. Early adolescence, encompassing the preteen years (ages 10 to 12-ish), is shaped by both the child's temperament and their preconceived notions about puberty. When parents send kids strong messages about adolescence ("You're going to be so moody when you're a teen" or "You'll be boy crazy next year"), kids often incorporate these ideas into their identity and manifest this behavior. Preteens may struggle with dishonesty, testing limits, and avoidance behavior. This can create tension between parents and preteens, and it may feel as if power struggles are a daily occurrence.

Middle adolescence, falling between the ages of 12 and 14-ish, covers the middle school years. Puberty is in full force and its physical and emotional changes result in impulsive behavior, curiosity about sex, and attention shifting away from family toward peers. Increased school demands require organization and task completion. Technology and social media begin to take precedence over other interests.

Late adolescence, spanning from age 15 to 18-ish, takes place during the high school years. At this point, teens' bodies begin to more closely resemble those of adults, but their undeveloped prefrontal cortexes contribute to risk taking, big emotions, and other distinctly adolescent behaviors. This is a time of particular stress for parents, as they watch their teen try to make good decisions despite the fact that they now have an adult body, a driver's license, considerably less supervision than they've ever had before, and a brain that leans toward impulsivity. Teens in this stage also tend to have an increased interest in romantic partnerships, so they need to learn how to create healthy boundaries.

Emerging adulthood, that span of time between high school graduation and the mid 20s, is the final hurdle between being a teen and being an adult. This stage of life is defined by exploration, as most young adults begin to consider their futures and make choices about their adult lives. Education, work, relationships, living circumstances, and leisure activities offer near-constant stimulation, so the emerging adult needs to figure out how to find their passions while also managing their adult responsibilities. During this time, the parent-child relationship often becomes more peaceful and can evolve into one more closely resembling friendship.

Don't Take It Personally— It's Science!

Our kids' brains do not reach the maximum potential until the kids are well into their 20s. This means that they will experience a significant amount of cognitive growth even after they can fit into size 12 shoes, drive a car in the snow, and solve calculus problems.

Our brains are *complex*. They're composed of about 100 billion nerve cells called neurons, which form networks and communicate with one another at a constant rate. Neurons send your body messages and demand that it respond accordingly. In fact, we're born with so many neurons that once our body masters a bunch of functional tasks, such as talking and walking, our brain prunes the redundant neurons to make room for the active, need-it-right-now neurons to expand.

One of the most unique aspects of youth brain development is *neuroplasticity*. Young brains alter themselves depending on what stimulation they are exposed to, in a quest to benefit from each new learning experience. For example, if during my childhood my parents give me piano lessons, take me to the opera, and jam out to music every time we're in the car, the neurons designated as "music neurons" in my brain are going to flourish. However, if they put me in a dark room at the age of six months and leave me there, my neurons are going to be stunted from understimulation and I will never learn to talk or see.

Environmental factors undoubtedly play a significant role in how children develop, especially regarding factors such as whether children are nurtured when they cry, if they are exposed to language and literacy at a young age, or if they experience physical trauma like a head injury or exposure to toxic chemicals. However, much of the behavior we see from our children and teens is determined by genetic makeup and typical brain development.

The upside of all of this is that we have a lot of influence over how our kids' brains develop. The downside is that while they are teens, their reasoning abilities, their emotional regulation, their ability to control impulses . . . sometimes are all a crapshoot, depending on which neurons are well developed enough to be useful in any given circumstance.

Here are some other interesting facts about brain development that might help you make more sense of the years to come:

→ The human brain begins to lose some memory abilities by the time an adult reaches their late 20s.

→ The human brain gets smaller as we get older.

→ Because about 75 percent of our brain is made up of water, even small amounts of dehydration can impair brain functions.

→ Using marijuana impacts the brain, causing problems in learning and memory, coordination, reaction time, and judgment.

Oh, the Drama!

Although there is so much to say about the emotional turmoil that teens experience, I think it's important to also pay attention to the feelings parents experience as our children grow up and away. It's super hard to watch your child transform from a little girl in pigtails to a young woman who uses contour makeup to accentuate her cleavage before she leaves to go on a date with the guy who was the catalyst for a conversation about birth control. Sometimes it feels like it physically hurts to separate from our children, especially knowing that they're going to get hurt, feel lonely, and hit us up for money at some point during their journey into adulthood. They'll fail at many things: exams, relationships, and being on time for important events, to name a few. Parents need to grieve a little, both for the child who once was and for the adolescent or young adult who now is, particularly if that adolescent is prickly, unpleasant, and full of bravado from feeling as if they know everything. They don't know everything. They just think they do, which is another failing of the adolescent brain.

It's also important to note that as teens prepare to leave the nest, they really don't understand the emotional journey their parents are on. They have no frame of reference for the ambivalence that parents feel, and as a result, teens can be impatient and unempathetic when their parents express sorrow or confusion about their offspring's insistence on autonomy and privacy. It's important that parents develop their own support system, because their adolescent is not likely to be a compassionate audience for their distress, nor is it the teen's role to be.

But right now, this is all in the future. Your child still loves being with you and talking to you, and will tolerate wearing the outfits you pick out for them. So enjoy it! Spend time appreciating their interests, whether that means stumbling through a video game, admiring puppy videos on the Internet, marveling as they jump into the pool over and over, or letting them help you in the kitchen. The traditions and routines that you create with them at this age may carry on during the teen years, when all your new ideas will immediately be viewed as annoying and lame.

Son, age 10 (points to a single hair on his toe): **Mom! I got The Puberty!**

Me: **I think we need to have another conversation about puberty, starting with not calling it THE puberty.**

Chapter Two

Early Adolescence:
Cute with a Side of 'Tude
(Ages 10-ish to 12-ish)

EARLY ADOLESCENCE TYPICALLY FALLS BETWEEN
the ages of 10 and 12. There is a lot of variability in how
kids, and therefore their parents, experience these years.
Some kids make their way through with little drama or
fanfare, taking their body's changes in stride, showing
grace toward the missteps of peers, and using the family
as a "home base" when they're frustrated, sad, or worried.
Other kids experience a bout of upheaval and begin
exhibiting increased irritability and high sensitivity to the
instability in their social world. They may also adopt perplexing behaviors, such as negative self-talk or avoidance
of hard or stressful things.

These differences in how kids respond to the inevitable creep of adolescence are primarily the result of two things:

1. **Your child's temperament:** If your child has always struggled with transitions, demonstrates changes in sleeping or eating habits when stressed, is quick to have big emotions over low-stress events, or is a "glass half empty" kind of kid, then they're more likely to have a stronger and more negative reaction to the uncertainty of preteenagerhood. If they are generally nonplussed by change, can express themselves in productive ways before big emotions take over, and aren't likely to take things personally when peers act inconsistently, then the preteen years should proceed with considerably less drama.

2. **Parents' response to the onset of puberty:** Some parents panic. They start talking about adolescence all the time, share inappropriate war stories ("Let me tell you about the time I got my period in math class and everyone called me 'Period Patty' until graduation"), and make assumptions that their kid is going to experience constant emotional upheaval. Though this is intended to soothe their child's worries, it can actually increase their anxiety about adolescence. Some parents also really struggle to separate from their kids during this time and, consequently, create a stressful push-pull relationship. Other parents, however, sprinkle tidbits about upcoming changes into conversations, rather than making them the focus of most conversations. They also take time to listen, give off a demeanor of "we'll figure out the tough moments together," and convey that mistakes are inevitable and okay. This kind of parenting is less likely to make children feel anxious about adolescence.

No matter what you think your child will think about their upcoming changes, it's crucial to educate your child about the changes BEFORE they start. Give kids strategies to deal with the changes prevalent during these years. It's also MUCH easier to talk about sex before kids get to the stage where they're mortified to say "fallopian tube" to their parent.

What's Going On? Characteristics Associated with Early Adolescence

Kids are going through tremendous changes during early adolescence. Although kids mature at different rates, there are some characteristics that are typical within the 10- to 12-year-old age range.

PHYSICALLY

Hormone changes occur in the brain as a precursor to the onset of puberty. Girls show physical signs of puberty approximately one to two years earlier than boys, usually in the form of a curvier figure, body hair, and their first period. Boys are unlikely to experience a significant increase in height during this stage but may develop body odor and suddenly need shoes that are three sizes larger. The grooming habits of early adolescents are variable; some preteens will become fascinated by adult grooming habits like wearing cologne or makeup, while others need to be nagged into showering twice a week. Early adolescents at this age still benefit from 9 to 11 hours of sleep, but their bedtime may naturally shift to a later time.

EMOTIONALLY

Self-esteem, or one's sense of self-worth, often takes a dip during early adolescence. Although early adolescents generally focus on their areas of strength, they are becoming more aware of the opinions of peers. They demonstrate ambivalence about growing up. While they may be interested in the fun aspects of getting older, like using a cell phone or staying home alone for short periods, they may also struggle with consistently exhibiting more mature behavior, such as studying on their own or starting dinner preparations before their parents get home from work. Early adolescents are very sensitive to perceived criticism and may still regularly have emotional outbursts that involve tears, yelling, or pouting. Adolescents in this age group have a strong sense of justice, feeling that fair means *equal*, and struggle to remain calm when they lose a competition or game.

SOCIALLY

Early adolescents tend to favor friendships with same-gender peers, as time spent with members of the opposite sex is accompanied by accusations of "liking them" (Eww!). Most of the time, children in this age group are very conscious of their actions around their peers and have learned to inhibit emotional outbursts. Much to their parents' disappointment, early adolescents may exhibit self-consciousness about showing affection toward their parents in public. While still very family focused, early adolescents gravitate toward activities with friends and may express a desire to be "popular." There is an increased interest in and dependence on social interaction through social media, live video games, and extracurricular activities.

A Serious Note About Early Puberty

Some kids begin to show signs of puberty earlier than their peers. Some girls may get their period in 4th or 5th grade, sprouting acne and developing breasts much earlier than their same-age peers; boys experiencing early puberty may develop broader shoulders, a crackly voice, and wisps of facial hair in 4th or 5th grade.

The fact is, early puberty is usually a positive experience for boys. Their increased height and weight can result in enhanced athletic ability and a physique that more closely matches their earlier-maturing female peers—all factors that can increase their popularity and self-esteem. In contrast, early-maturing girls are more likely to socialize with other youths who are in the same stage of puberty, potentially exposing them to "older kid" behaviors like drinking, illegal drugs, and sexual activity. The combination of underdeveloped prefrontal cortex and maturing body can be a tough mix, and impulsive, poorly considered behaviors are more likely. These girls are at risk of experiencing low self-esteem, shame, anxiety, and depression, especially if they come from homes with harsh or uninvolved parenting. Parents should be on the lookout for their child engaging in negative self-talk, receiving unwelcome attention from older teens, being sad, withdrawing from previously enjoyed activities, or practicing secretive online activity. They can also offer early-maturing girls close supervision, a listening ear, affection, and plenty of opportunities for parent-child time and social interaction with their typically developing peers.

What to Expect

Early adolescence generally occurs from the end of elementary school through the transition into middle school—a time of significant change. In school, kids have more independence, need to learn to balance the personalities and expectations of multiple teachers, and use technology to both study and keep in touch with their friends. Social demands have magnified; the desire to fit in has intensified, and kids' newfound habit of comparing themselves to their peers may impact their self-esteem. Parents have a reduced role in managing their child's social life and are now tasked with teaching more responsibility and independence, and setting the groundwork for their child's teenage years.

This is a tough stage because, as parents, we're not sure how to react. When our early adolescents make poor decisions, should we show compassion and leeway because they're learning and growing? Or should we be worried about sending a message that their behavior is acceptable, and thus ushering in the opportunity for more troublesome behavior during the teen years? Here are a few examples of the most common challenges faced by parents of early adolescents, along with suggestions on how to address them.

DISHONESTY

In my work with families, I've seen parents become extremely distressed when their child exhibits dishonesty, such as lying, cheating, or omitting information, especially if it appears to be a pattern of behavior. Oftentimes parents catastrophize dishonest behavior, assuming that their child has a glaring character flaw, that they've failed as parents, and that their child is destined to become a criminal and end up in prison. None of these things are true.

Why Do Kids Lie So Much?

Kids lie for a variety of reasons, most notably the following:

1. **To avoid getting in trouble:** They may deny that they broke their laptop or claim that a teacher wasn't available for help after school.

2. **To avoid something unpleasant:** They may be avoiding nagging from a parent or an awkward interaction with a peer.

3. **To avoid shame or embarrassment:** They may minimize a health concern or avoid revealing something they're not good at.

4. **To protect privacy or keep a secret:** They may delete texts or deny involvement in a social activity.

5. **To control someone's impression of them:** They may wish to appear popular, smart, or successful in order to preserve their self-esteem or to prevent someone from being disappointed in them.

6. **To be or feel safe:** They may give untruthful statements to protect their safety, such as "My mom is on her way to pick me up" or "My dad won't let me go."

When it comes to our children, we tend to view them as falling in one of two categories: a truthful person or an untruthful person. In reality, no one, especially parents, falls into only one category, because lying is an extremely complex form of communication. There are times when lying might even be considered functional, such as when Grandma asks your teen how they liked the extremely dorky "Someone in Tampa Loves Me" sweatshirt she sent them ("It's so cute!").

There are also times when lying is dangerous, is mean-spirited, or causes long-term consequences. Examples of destructive lying might include denying participation in unsafe behavior (touching a gun found in a drawer at a peer's house), misleading someone to be spiteful (telling a peer that everyone at school hates her), or creating a negative long-term consequence (throwing out a needed medication rather than taking it).

Being truthful often requires delaying gratification and sitting in a place of discomfort in the hope that it will pay off eventually. This is tough for preteens and teens. They may not want to stop playing video games to finish studying or go brush their teeth, so they simply lie and say they already did it. Conversations about the complexity of lying and the importance of truthfulness should be frequent but brief, and they should be applied to as many real-life scenarios as possible.

How to Help If Your Early Adolescent Is Struggling with Dishonesty

There's no one-size-fits-all approach for dealing with this behavior when it inevitably occurs. Ideally, parents should have an ongoing discussion about lying and general honesty, because it's going to take extensive support for kids to understand the nuances. Making a global family rule of "you should never lie" or "all lying is bad" is unrealistic, because there are occasions when parents lie and when lying might be functional, as mentioned previously. Instead, it would be helpful to discuss lying in terms of integrity and taking responsibility for your own behavior.

It should also be recognized that lying is a very normalized behavior in our society. Kids, teens, and adults often believe that lying can be justified if it allows them to get ahead. Nearly every TV show, even shows designed for kids, creates conflict via lying. In addition, everyone gets away with lying on occasion. This, by nature, is very reinforcing. Given this reality, it's important to set an expectation in your home about lying. This means that you're going to have to reflect on and discuss your own experiences of lying, especially when your kid observes it, and decipher whether it upholds the family standard.

Here are some strategies to use when your kid lies:

1. **Stay calm.** Nothing is to be gained by you losing your cool, engaging in a discussion of global character flaws, or refusing to listen to the child's version of the truth.

2. **Recognize that there may be more than one version of the truth.** You may have a different interpretation than your child, because you have a grown-up brain, are privy to different information, or have a different emotional response. In client sessions, I often learn that the parent's belief about the lying behavior doesn't correspond with the child's perspective of the situation. It's difficult to find a solution if both parties have completely different impressions of the event.

3. **Don't assume they know why they've lied.** Your child may not have the cognitive skills to be self-reflective, or they may have lied without forethought. There is a decent chance that if you ask your kid why they lied, they're going to say, "I don't know," and be sincere.

4. **Don't take lying personally.** Your kid is not lying just to make you feel like a failure as a parent. There is a purpose behind it, and oftentimes it has nothing to do with you.

5. **Help them figure out the words to use when they need to tell you about a mistake.** We often tell kids not to lie because "you can tell me anything." But we don't always give them the words to tell us about a mistake, so they resort to lying and then the focus is shifted to the lie rather than the original mistake. After an incident, try reenacting the scenario. Switch roles and have the parent role-play an appropriate way for the kid to confess to a mistake, and the kid portray how they would prefer the parent respond to the information.

Parent: I asked you if you used my cell phone without permission, didn't I? Because I found it with a cracked screen? You said you didn't, which was untruthful.
Kid: Yeah.
Parent: Okay, you be me, I'll be you. Let's try this again without lying.
Kid: Okay.
Parent (role-playing the kid): Mom, I made a huge mistake, and I think you're going to be upset about it.
Kid (role-playing the parent): What did you do?
Parent: I used your phone without permission. I dropped it and the screen broke. I'm so sorry!
Kid: Oh no! I told you not to use my phone. I'm so angry!
Parent: I know. I'm really sorry. I didn't mean to break it.
Kid: I'm glad you told me the truth, and I'm glad you apologized. You might have to help me pay for a new screen. I still feel really upset.

6. **Give consequences.** If circumstances around your kid's lying go against your family expectations, explain your reasons, describe what they should have

done instead, and give a consequence that makes sense to the situation. For example, if they lied about doing their homework, institute a policy where they complete their homework at the kitchen table each night before they have access to technology, and do a daily or weekly check-in of their grades on the student portal.

7. **Ask less, confirm more.** If your child seems to be lying chronically, spend less time asking for the facts, and simply assess the situation and then give an instruction. Rather than asking if they've taken out the trash, just check to see if it's been done. If it hasn't, instruct them to do it. You may need to suggest a consequence to ensure they feel a sense of investment in complying with your instructions, such as no more video games for the evening if they don't take care of the trash.

8. **Understand why kids lie.** One of the primary reasons that kids lie is because adults set the stage for it. When parents ask their kid a question about their behavior even though they already know the answer, kids will often shift into a lie that could potentially salvage the parent's goodwill or prevent a punishment. This can end in angry confrontations, accusations that you know your child is a liar, and misery all around. Instead, we can work to avoid creating a situation in which kids are tempted to lie.

Mom (using her family GPS app to see that her son is at a friend's house 15 minutes away, even though she asked him to be home in 10 minutes for dinner): **Hey, bud. I see from the GPS app that you're not on your way home yet. I was expecting you at 6:00 p.m.**

Son: Oh no! I lost track of time while playing video games. I'll get my stuff together and leave here within five minutes. I'll hurry, but I know I'm going to be at least 10 minutes late. I'm sorry.

Mom: It's okay. I'll see you soon. When you get home, we'll think of a strategy you can use to remind yourself when to head home.

Son: 'K. Leaving now!

Say This, Not That!

In this scenario, Mom calmly let her son know that she was aware that he was going to be late and encouraged him to comply with her new directive (come home now). She also accepted his apology gracefully, which can be another challenge for parents. She focused on helping him not repeat the mistake instead of punishing him. Here are some more suggestions on how to foster truthful communication between parent and early adolescent:

SAY THIS	NOT THAT
I want to ask you a question, and I want you to concentrate on being truthful. Take your time and think before you answer.	What the heck happened? When I find out who did this, they're going to be in so much trouble!
I want you to tell me the truth. I'm going to try to stay calm, but I can't promise I won't be angry or disappointed.	You can always tell me the truth and I'll never get mad.
Let's start this conversation over from the beginning. I already know what really happened, so please don't be tempted to be untruthful.	You are a liar. People don't like or trust liars.

TESTING LIMITS

Testing limits, or resisting boundaries or rules that parents have established, is an essential part of growing up. In fact, most conflicts in families with preteens and teens stem from arguments about daily rules and routines (chores, curfew, bedtime, technology) rather than big-ticket items (safety, religious or political beliefs, or overall values). When a child experiments with testing limits, it's usually the first sign that parents need to modify their boundaries to better correspond with their child's development.

Why Early Adolescents Test Limits

Testing limits, while frustrating for parents, is age-appropriate behavior. Early adolescents want access to more privileges and to spend more time with their peers, so they begin to protest the boundaries established by parents during their younger years. If parents respond quickly, consistently, and compassionately to limit-testing, this behavior is unlikely to escalate beyond what is typical of growing adolescents.

In my experience, there are three primary predictors of whether kids will develop chronic limit-testing behavior:

1. **Poor communication is role modeled by a parent or caregiver.** This may begin with parents nagging, lecturing, or threatening consequences. If they don't get the results desired, they begin yelling, then swiftly progress to verbal disrespect. Parents might say things like:

   "What's wrong with you?"
   "Every other kid can do this. Why can't you?"
   "I never acted this way when I was a kid."
   "Shut up and do what I told you to do."

"I'm sick of you."
"Get out of my sight."
"I don't know what to do with you."
"Fine. Go live with your dad/grandparent."

Some of you might find these words shocking, and some of you may nod ruefully, hearing your own voice in those words. While your kid may not mirror those exact words back to you, you may recognize the tone or spirit behind these words. For most people, parents and children alike, words like these mean "I'm giving up on you," "You're irredeemable," "I don't want to be around you," "It would be easier if I didn't have to deal with you." Hearing those messages from a family member is destructive to a child's sense of self-worth and a parent's sense of competence and investment in parenting.

2. **Kids are mimicking poor communication from television, movies, video games, social media, and peers.** If you're hearing a lot of ugly words and an ugly tone come out of your youth's mouth, and you feel certain they are not mirroring you or another adult, do some investigation. What music are they listening to? What video games are they playing? What television shows do they find most relatable? Some kids are excellent at understanding that they shouldn't imitate everything they hear, but others just soak it right in and absorb it as part of their own identity. Your child may need to have limited exposure to these types of influences until they have enough practice understanding how to use appropriate language.

3. **Kids are not given appropriate consequences for using this negative language.** Instead, parents tend to react by giving in (reacting to their child's demands or

negative outbursts by responding in their favor), escalating (becoming incensed by their child's language and tone, making the interaction more explosive), or getting defensive (overexplaining their rationale for a certain directive or rule).

How to Help When Your Early Adolescent Begins to Test Limits

Testing limits often takes the form of negotiation, verbal disrespect, and noncompliance. Each of these presents its own challenges.

1. **Stand firm when they try negotiation.** Negotiation usually takes the form of bargaining, protesting and proposing another option, or arguing. Negotiation can be exhausting for parents, as it often results in a back-and-forth conversation that can become belligerent. It's important to note that negotiation, if gone unchecked, can be a significant contributor to kids generally feeling discontent, because they're always focusing on the next best thing rather than being present in the moment.

    Parent: **Kiddo, turn off the PlayStation and go shower and get ready for bed.**
    Early adolescent: **I'm at the most important part of the game! Everyone is depending on me!**
    Parent: **It's 8:30 p.m. That's the deal. Turn it off, please.**
    Early adolescent: **Ten more minutes! No, five more minutes! C'mon! Please!**
    Parent: **Turn it off or you're not going to be given the opportunity to use it tomorrow.**
    Early adolescent: **Ugh! This is so unfair! No one else has to stop playing!**

Minimizing your child's motivation to *negotiate* is best achieved by having consistent rules *and* by having a process to discuss modification of the rules. If you can be worn down, manipulated, or made to feel guilty and cave in to their demands, then negotiation will be reinforced. Kids are going to capitalize on that. In contrast, if kids feel that rules are not appropriate for their age or circumstance, be open to a discussion, *but not in the moment.* Encourage them to schedule a time to discuss it later when everyone is calm and can engage in discussion, collaboration, and compromise.

Recently, my 12-year-old son wanted to present his case as to why he should be allowed to get dropped off at an amusement park on a Friday night with some friends, without any adult chaperones. He asked to speak with me before bedtime, shared his reasoning in a calm voice, and encouraged me to think it over. We later decided that he would be allowed to go to the amusement park if he met a number of expectations beforehand: finding a strategy to carry his phone so it wouldn't get lost in the park, demonstrating for at least two weeks that he would consistently keep his ringer on and answer immediately when a parent called, and only choosing to go with friends who already had experience with spending time in public places and consistently made good choices. The expectations were clearly stated prior to modifying the rule.

2. **Help them label their emotions and find better words when they engage in verbal disrespect.** Verbal disrespect is one of the most infuriating ways that kids push boundaries. It's a type of communication that

hovers between appropriate communication and verbal abuse, and parents often have a hard time recognizing the nuances between them. Some parents simply consider this to be "teenager talk" and normalize it, assuming that all kids speak this way. Yes, all preteens and teens are going to test limits by using language that's saltier than necessary, but it's important that parents set a standard for how family members speak to one another so verbal disrespect doesn't become the norm. In my work with families, we often spend time clarifying the difference between kids expressing negative emotions appropriately and verbal disrespect—namely, that verbal disrespect is not focused on conveying emotion, but rather is intended to be hurtful or emotionally manipulative.

Expressing negative emotions looks something like this:

"Mom, this is so unfair!"
"I hate this rule."
"You don't understand me."

In contrast, verbal disrespect sounds like:

"You are the worst mom ever!"
"I don't care what you think!"
"I wish you weren't my dad!"

Some parents get a little prickly when their kid expresses negative emotions, labeling it as disrespect, taking it personally, or viewing it as a sign of ungratefulness. However, kids who express their emotions in a socially appropriate manner tend to have better developed emotional regulation, self-advocacy skills, and self-competence. Verbal disrespect, however, should be limited. Early adolescence comes with some big emotions. Youths need to understand that while expressing emotions is healthy and productive, using words as weapons will not lead to privileges or autonomy. It will take a lot of practice to navigate these emotions, and parents will have to be very involved in the process.

Kids who are engaging in verbal disrespect can often identify that they feel bad but can't articulate a specific feeling or reasoning behind it, so it can be valuable to help them label the emotions ("You sound frustrated." "Are you feeling disappointed?").

Once a negative feeling is identified, help them figure out how to cope with it in a proactive way. Tactics might include having them take a break in their room, listen to music, meditate, exercise, spend time with a pet, talk it out, or problem solve by asking an adult for help.

When kids say something disrespectful, we often say, "Don't talk to me like that!" or "Watch your mouth!" but we don't give them a script for what to say instead. For example, instead of saying, "You're the meanest mom ever," they can say, "I'm so upset and this feels unfair."

3. **Give them consequences if they keep engaging in verbal disrespect.** Kids should be reminded that they can't have "big kid" privileges without demonstrating corresponding big kid behavior. Privileges such as using technology, going on sleepovers, or being given pocket money should be based on their effort to handle the tougher moments, like being told no or managing a negative emotion. In my work,

I consistently encourage kids and parents to "practice the no." This means that parents need to say no (and avoid indulging) when their kids demonstrate verbal disrespect, and kids need to learn to deal with the no when they hear it (stay calm and accept their parent's decision).

4. **Set reasonable rules and consequences if they are noncompliant.** Noncompliance, or the refusal to comply with an adult's directions, can take two forms: passive noncompliance and active non-compliance. Passive noncompliance occurs when you ask your child to do something and they just . . . don't do it. You get home from work and the dish-washer isn't emptied. You tell them to study for their math test and their book isn't even opened. They don't verbally refuse or speak disrespectfully. They just don't do what you've asked. In contrast, active noncompliance occurs when you ask your child to do something and they verbally state their noncompliance, saying something like "No" or "I don't have to listen to you." Don't shift the expec-tation to something less demanding, bribe them into complying, or doubt your judgment because your child is upset. State your expectation, clearly describe the consequences, and let the chips fall where they may. Prior to verbalizing consequences, consider them carefully. Parents are often tempted to pile on more severe consequences in the moment because they're angry or hoping to pressure their child into complying.

Parent: **I'd like you to take the dog out for a walk.**
Early adolescent: **No, I don't feel like it.**

Parent: **We've talked about this. If I ask you to do something to be helpful around the house and you refuse, you will lose your access to video games for the rest of the day.**

Early adolescent: **I don't care. I'm not walking the dog.**

Parent: **Fine. Then you've lost your video games *and* your phone.**

Early adolescent: **What?! That's crap!**

Parent: **And for using that language, the TV is getting turned off, too!**

Now you're in a power struggle, tempers are hot, and your child may be enjoying your extreme reaction. And once everyone is calm an hour later, it's tempting to shift back to the original punishment, which was well thought out and probably more appropriate, and the child inadvertently gets rewarded for their noncompliance. Once you've decided upon an appropriate consequence, don't second-guess yourself in the moment.

Say This, Not That!

Although limit-testing is to be expected, parents can greatly influence how disruptive it is to home life. If testing limits works for kids—that is, if it gets them their desired results—then it's going to continue and most likely intensify. Staying calm is key, because kids will take their cues from parents when it comes to managing emotions. Some helpful phrases to respond with when your adolescent is pushing your buttons may include the following:

SAY THIS	NOT THAT
We've already talked about this. I know you're disappointed, but my answer hasn't changed.	I'll say it again. You can't _____ because _____, _____, and _____!
I know you're angry, but you're using disrespectful language. If you're angry, say, "Dad, I'm angry." Don't call people names.	Don't talk to me like that! You're acting like a spoiled brat! Who do you think you are?
We'll talk about this when you're calm.	You've just lost use of your Xbox for the weekend! Now it's a full week! Now it's two weeks! Keep going, and it'll be a month!

Verbal abuse is anything that includes name-calling, threats, or curse words that are directed toward someone. Examples may include "I'm going to make you sorry you did that" or "You're a bitch." Repeated incidents of verbal abuse (or more worrisome, physical aggression) should be addressed immediately via family counseling, individual counseling, or parent coaching. Additionally, parents need to look closely at their own communication style and make sure it isn't setting a precedent for their child. This is a difficult dynamic to resolve without professional help.

ANXIETY AND AVOIDANCE

In today's society, youth anxiety is at an all-time high, with approximately 30 percent of kids under 18 exhibiting symptoms severe enough to warrant a clinical diagnosis. Some symptoms are overt: poor sleep, changes in appetite, trembling, panic attacks, crying, hiding, fleeing the environment, and verbally expressing worry and fear. Others are more subtle and may be attributed to other factors: irritability, clingy behavior, sensitivity, withdrawal, slow reactivity, argumentativeness, or a need for constant reassurance. While anxiety is prevalent in nearly all age groups, it can be difficult to identify in early adolescents because (a) anxiety takes so many different forms and early adolescents are not skilled at recognizing or articulating it, and (b) it often manifests itself as avoidance, which is a red herring for well-intentioned parents. Anxiety, and the subsequent avoidance behavior, is so commonplace that it's difficult to know if these symptoms are just a typical part of growing up or if they're a sign of something more concerning.

Some anxiety is functional. It helps keep us safe, like when we remain alert while walking across a parking lot. It triggers effort, like when we proofread our essay before turning it in. It keeps us socially aware, like when we look for signs that someone thinks our joke was funny. But too much anxiety incapacitates both kids and parents. In parents, anxiety often makes them think of worst-case scenarios: "He's never going to get into college and is going to live at home until he's 35," "How did I raise a kid who could bully a peer? What did I do wrong?," or "My friend's kid knows how to play guitar; we've never even encouraged her in music." We put pressure on our kids because of our own fears and insecurities, and this is unfair and counterproductive to our relationship with our children.

Why Are Early Adolescents So Anxious?
Some of the most stressful aspects of a preteen's life, especially as they're entering middle school, are the academic and organizational demands of school. Dealing

with the various demands and personalities of multiple teachers, managing academic materials, studying and adhering to timelines, advocating for themselves if they have a special learning need, etc. are all stressful, and it just gets worse as adults remind kids that high school "will be here before you know it."

At this age, kids are just starting to form an academic identity. Is it cool to be smart? Is their self-esteem at least partially dependent on their grades? Are they well liked by teachers? Do they have a sense of the future yet? If so, is it dependent upon their school competence? Do they identify themselves as a student first or does their primary sense of self come from their athletic prowess or social standing?

The other primary source of stress in a preteen's life is their *perception* of connectedness to their peer group. Notice I wrote *perception*. Early adolescents, while still extraordinarily attached to their family members, are gaining more satisfaction from being around peers who they feel are fun and interesting. With this desire to be with their peers comes a hyperawareness of how their peers view them. However, preteens don't necessarily have an accurate perception of their social standing. Some kids are oblivious to the fact that peers find them abrasive or immature. Other kids are well liked and generally accepted, but feel like outcasts if one admired peer doesn't return their friendly advances. Some kids handle teasing well and interpret it as a form of inclusion to the group, but others fall down a well of negative self-talk and respond by self-isolating.

True self-esteem evolves from working toward a goal and making progress or succeeding. Therefore, effort should be praised ("You worked so hard on your project, how fantastic!") instead of basic ability ("You're so smart"). This reinforces to kids that (a) effort and practice are important and (b) they're in control of their progress.

How to Help If Your Early Adolescent Is Struggling with Avoidance

Avoidance, as mentioned previously, is one of the most common indicators that a preteen is experiencing anxiety. It occurs when the sense of being overwhelmed surpasses feelings of industry, and kids become frozen, unable to activate themselves enough to make progress toward a goal. Basically, they use avoidance to cope with feeling bombarded by demands, even if these demands appear to be small or low stress. It's a strategy that is very effective short-term, but often has some pretty hefty long-term consequences.

Avoidance behavior results in stagnation, which is extraordinarily frustrating to parents. Here are some suggestions to conquer avoidance behavior in early adolescence:

1. **Prioritize.** Focus on what you can control. For example, you can't *make* your child study. You can, however, hire a tutor. You can allow them to download some educational apps. You can help them access the class website. You can inform their teacher that your child

is struggling. You can give consequences to your child for earning poor grades. You can create an environment conducive to studying. But you can't actually *force* your child to do unenforceable things, like study, sleep, eat healthy, or enjoy doing something. Make sure you're focusing your energy and resources on aspects of your child and their environment that you *can* control.

2. **Don't tell them how they feel.** "You just don't care about school." "You never think about anyone else." People of all ages have complex feelings and they feel alienated, misunderstood, and disconnected when others make assumptions about how they feel. Ask your kid how they feel. Let them know what feeling you're tempted to attribute to them when you observe their behavior. Listen to their response.

Dad: **You have to clean your room by bedtime tonight, or you lose your phone for the rest of the weekend.**
Teen: **Fine, okay.**
Dad (several hours later): **Hey, it's almost bedtime and you haven't picked up a single sock in this room! You're just scrolling on your phone! What's going on? It seems like you don't even care.**
Teen: **I just . . . I looked at my room, and it seemed like cleaning it up was impossible! And I knew I was going to get my phone taken away anyway. There's no way I'd do a good enough job to keep it. I just didn't know what to do.**

3. **Cue, don't nag.** Preteens' and teens' executive functioning skills, or ability to prioritize, plan, initiate, control impulses, and remain organized, are significantly less

well developed than they'll be when the kids are in their mid 20s. So kids need to be cued. They need to be taught how to use strategies, and they need to be reinforced when they do a good job. This reinforcement could take the form of verbal praise, physical affection (hug, fist bump), access to a privilege (use of a cell phone, permission to host a sleepover with a friend), or a tangible item (candy, gift card for a favorite store).

However tempting it is to nag, it's important to understand that *it's just not helpful.* If anything, it contributes to kids becoming more dependent on their parents. Kids tend to develop the attitude of "I'll just keep doing nothing until her nagging turns to yelling and I know I'll get in serious trouble." Instead of nagging, ask how you can support them. Help them devise a plan and break it into manageable parts. Reinforce them when they've achieved a goal. Accept when they need to fail to learn.

Parent: I just wanted to remind you that it's 8:00 p.m. You need to have your homework done and be showered by 9:00 p.m.
Adolescent (doesn't move): Okay.
Parent: I'd like you to turn off your video game now so you can get everything done. Finish your homework first, and then take a shower. Plan to be in the shower by 8:40 p.m.
Adolescent (still isn't moving): Uh-huh.
Parent: If the video game is distracting you from getting your responsibilities done, then let's plan to put it away tomorrow.

4. **Let them fail.** Sometimes the best way to decrease avoidance behavior is to allow kids to see the consequences of it. This may require letting them fail a class, lose a privilege, disappoint a teacher, or go without a necessary object or material.

Parent: I checked your grades online and you have three homework assignments with zeros.
Adolescent: Yeah.
Parent: Can you tell me what happened?
Adolescent: I did two of them, but I forgot to turn them in. I just forgot to do the last one.
Parent: Have you thought of a plan to deal with the zeros?
Adolescent: I think we're allowed to turn in assignments late and get half credit.
Parent: Makes sense. Do you have a strategy so you can remember to turn in the completed assignments tomorrow?
Adolescent: I don't know. Maybe I can put them in the front of my notebook so I'll see them when it's time to take notes in class.
Parent: Okay. Try that. How about turning them in first thing in the morning when I drop you off in the car rider line? Would that help?
Adolescent: Maybe, yes.

Say This, Not That!

Learning how to problem solve is a powerful tool to combat anxiety. It's easy to become frozen when you're overwhelmed, which results in feelings of helplessness and incompetence. Here are some suggestions about how to effectively communicate with your adolescent and encourage effective problem-solving skills when they're demonstrating anxious or avoidant behavior:

SAY THIS	NOT THAT
Let's figure out what you can do to deal with this problem.	You should know better.
Now that we've come up with a strategy, what do you think the consequence should be if you don't follow through?	You'll be sorry if you don't fix this mess.
I feel like you're having a hard time getting started. I'd like you to think about what you're feeling.	What is wrong with you? Just do what you're supposed to do.
I feel like you might be getting overwhelmed. Let's stop and just start with step 1.	Stop being so lazy.

Limit or Let Go

How do you give your kids the room to safely explore their limits, while also keeping them safe and emphasizing respect? Here are a few ideas:

LIMIT	LET GO
Screen time	Selfies
Disrespect	The occasional "LMAO" or "WTF" that you see in their text messages to their peers
Unsupervised time with friends, especially in groups	Alone time in their room
Gossip	Off-handed comparisons about themselves versus peers
Negative self-talk	Focus on appearances

Me: **What's the best part of transitioning from 7th to 8th grade?**

Daughter (thoughtfully): **I got boobs.**

Chapter Three

Middle Adolescence:
Less Cute, More Puberty
(Ages 12-ish to 14-ish)

MIDDLE ADOLESCENCE, WHICH TYPICALLY FALLS between the ages of 12 and 14, is primarily experienced during the middle school years. Often reported as one of the most stressful stages of development for both parents and kids, middle adolescence is largely shaped by the physical, emotional, and social consequences of puberty. Within this span of time, kids shed their physical vestiges of childhood, trading clear skin and snuggles on the couch for body hair, overactive sweat glands, and moods that are as variable as the clothes they wear.

Parents may get trapped in a merry-go-round, attempting to balance their teen's desire to explore and develop independence with their simultaneous need for guidance and support. One day, your teen seems to be rocking it—managing school demands, trying new things, and connecting with peers—while the next day they have a string of zeros in their grade book and complain "no one likes me." Parents need to take a deep breath and recognize that this comes with the territory as their child moves toward adulthood.

What's Going On? Characteristics Associated with Middle Adolescence

PHYSICALLY

Puberty causes a physical transformation. In girls, puberty typically starts with a burst of height, breast development, and pubic hair growth. About six months to a year after these changes are initiated, girls are likely to experience their first period. Some girls proceed through puberty at a slow and even pace, and others undergo it rapidly. For example, breast development takes an average of four years, but some girls are fully developed within two years, and others take up to nine years. Within a few months after a girl experiences her first period, her growth typically slows and stops. By the time a girl completes middle school, she's typically reached her adult height and her figure resembles that of a grown woman.

Boys, in contrast, don't typically show outward signs of puberty until near the end of middle school. While puberty typically starts with the growth of the penis and testes, it's the growth spurt of up to eight inches, the deepening voice, and the development of body hair that are the most noticeable changes. Most significantly, there is a sharp increase in muscle mass, apparent in a widening chest, broader shoulders, and a more muscular frame. During this time, parents notice an increase in food intake, physical awkwardness, sweating, and acne. Testosterone is a powerful hormone, and it's the driving force behind boys' puberty.

EMOTIONALLY

Puberty also causes a psychological transformation. Understandably, teens are going to have an emotional reaction to the physical changes their body is undergoing. In fact, research indicates that being generally happy about one's appearance is the most significant factor in determining a teen's self-esteem. Weight is often linked to girls' degree of contentment because many girls covet being thin. In contrast, a growing number of boys are preoccupied with developing a muscular frame. Societal pressures, interest in sports and other activities that value leanness, as well as genetic and biological factors can contribute to preoccupation with weight and body image.

SOCIALLY

With the development of a more mature body comes the desire to socialize in ways that are also more adult. Boys and girls begin to have mixed-gender social circles, a hierarchy begins to develop (the popular crowd versus the nonpopular crowd), and social connections are defined by proximity, common interests, and access to social media.

Brain Change

During middle adolescence, brain changes are largely governed by the sex hormones. In girls, progesterone and estrogen fluctuate in tandem with the menstrual cycle. In boys, testosterone can surge to up to 30 times its prepuberty amount. Because these sex hormones are linked to mood, and adolescents are inexperienced at dealing with these hormonal changes, they can result in a teen who demonstrates mood instability, sensation seeking, or even aggression. Despite the fact that these teens physically resemble adults, it's important to remember that they are not adults; their brains are still immature, they haven't mastered how to regulate emotions and impulses, and they still need guidance to stay organized, plan ahead, and recall important tasks and expectations.

What to Expect

Parents report that adolescents in this age range have a sharp increase in worldly knowledge. As these kids leave behind elementary school and enter middle school, they go from being the oldest kids in the group to the youngest, and suddenly they're exposed to a myriad of experiences that quickly transform their knowledge base. Kids are inundated very quickly with curse words; sexual terms; school instruction in current events of a sensitive nature; mature content in music, on television, and online; and it goes on. A 12-year-old client once told me that one of the most shocking aspects of transitioning to middle school was the degree to which middle schoolers used curse words, especially when adults weren't around. Within weeks he indicated that he barely noticed it anymore and occasionally used those words himself. Combining the onset of puberty with the exposure to more mature content and social interactions causes considerable changes in friendships, self-concept, boundary setting, and the desire to be more independent with daily tasks and routines. Kids become preoccupied with how others view them, and often their perspective is skewed by inaccurate assumptions, self-doubt, and exaggerated emotions.

FRIENDSHIPS AND SOCIAL PRESSURE

During middle adolescence, the social dynamic changes drastically. Kids are no longer interested in primarily socializing with same-sex peers, they prefer contact with friends over family, and social media has a significant influence on their ideas about their own likability and connectedness. Friendships are more complex, moving beyond relationships simply with those who live nearby or share similar interests. Middle adolescents are still learning how to be good friends, how to navigate the push and pull of peer expectations, and how to manage divided loyalties and the uncertainty of potential romantic partnerships.

Why Do Teens Struggle So Much with Social Dynamics?

Developing and maintaining friendships can be challenging for young teens, because they have not yet developed their identity as social beings. Are they an introvert or extrovert? Do they have a stronger need to be popular or to experience emotional closeness with one or two people? Do they struggle to trust others? Do they covet excessive attention from peers? Do they know how to teach people how to treat them? What's the difference between having an argument with a friend and being a participant in a toxic friendship? These questions aren't all going to be answered at this age—or possibly ever—but it's important to recognize that the combination of your teen's individual characteristics and the complexity of the social world they live in can be confusing and difficult to manage.

Some factors to consider when trying to understand teen friendships draw us back to what we know about the underdeveloped teenage brain:

1. **Lack of impulse control:** Words and phrases kids often use to describe middle school friendships include *drama, frenemies, trying to act cool, just wanting to be popular,* and *trying to impress a crush.* Relational aggression—hostile acts designed to cause harm to a person's relationship with another person—is rampant. Teens have trouble with the long game when it comes to friendships. They tend to act in ways that are responsive to the immediate situation without recognizing that a short-term behavior, such as lashing out, saying something that they don't mean, and even acting cruel, could cause long-term damage to a friendship or to their reputation. It's tempting to label this behavior as a character flaw, but it's more accurate to consider it an impulsive act born of immaturity and a temporary failure to consider the feelings of others. However, it's important that these incidents are addressed quickly and decisively so that the teen can learn from the incident and grow as a friend.

2. **Lack of self-regulation:** Teens are not known for remaining calm during moments of stress. They often irrationally assume that the worst-case scenario

is certain to occur. With these irrational thoughts comes an exaggerated emotional response. Imagine the teen who opens her social media account and learns that some of her friends had a sleepover without her. She may immediately respond with magnified emotions and thoughts such as "Those girls aren't my friends. They probably all sat around and talked about me behind my back. They were probably laughing at me and they think I'm a loser." These thoughts are accompanied by emotions such as loneliness, anxiety, humiliation, and feelings of negative self-worth. Impulsively, she posts a picture of the hostess of the party with a big X over her face and writes, "Wonder if her crush, Benjamin, knows how much she likes him? Spoke to him yesterday and he said, 'No way.'" Within moments, this post has been viewed by dozens of classmates and Benjamin texts, "WTF?" with an angry-face emoji. Lines are drawn. Suddenly this teen's social standing has been completely altered, and almost immediately she's filled with regret.

How to Help Your Adolescent Deal with Friendship Struggles

Watching your teen deal with the uncertainty and emotional roller coaster of transient friendships can be heartbreaking. Most of us can recall the despair we felt as teens, and these feelings are magnified when we consider the relentlessness of social media and the Internet. But there are steps you can take to help.

1. **Offer compassion.** It's important to offer compassion and understanding for your teen and their emotional reaction to social pressures, because peer relationships are likely to be one of the top stressors in your teen's life. At times, parents might feel impatient

("OMG, they're seriously arguing about that boy again?"), indignant ("Kaley said what? What a brat!"), or even angry ("I'm calling his mother to see if she knows what kind of son she has"). But even if you're struggling with the fact that your child is clearly hurting, focus on being a good listener and letting your child explain their perspective and their process of solving the problem. They may be open to suggestions later in the conversation, or might just need to feel heard. Either way, try not to muddy the waters by inserting your own emotional response.

Parent: I heard you yell something while you were on the phone with Jesse. What's up?
Son: He always tries to act cool during lunch.
Parent: What do you mean by that?
Son: He'll, like, mock me. Usually about my height. He only does it when Mark and Jacob are around, because he thinks it makes him look cool.
Parent: Did you tell him how you felt?
Son: Yeah, I told him that if he's going to be a jerk at lunch, he shouldn't call me later and act like we're best friends.
Parent: How'd it go when you said that to him?
Son: I don't know. I ended up yelling at him and just sort of hung up.

2. **Encourage the teen to focus on what they can control.**
Helping teens identify what they can and cannot control in a social situation can provide them with a powerful tool. Things that teens cannot control include how others feel and how others behave.

Things that teens can control include how they interpret or reframe a situation, how they respond verbally or physically (what they do with their body, such as body language, showing an angry response, or walking away), whether they ask for help from a trusted adult, what choices they make on the Internet or social media, whom they choose to surround themselves with in the future, and how they choose to represent their personal values when dealing with other people.

Parent: So, you've told your friend how you feel. What do you think you might do next?
Son: I might text him later. Tell him I'm not upset anymore.
Parent: How do you think he'll respond?
Son: I don't know. He might be mad that I yelled at him. Or he might feel bad that I was mad at him.
Parent: What will you say if he's angry or if he doesn't answer your text?
Son: I'll probably just give him some time. I think we'll probably be cool again by tomorrow.
Parent: What will you do if he continues to tease you during lunch?
Son: I don't know. I might plan to go sit with some other friends for a few days.

3. **Help them learn how to not take things personally.** There is a lot going on in an adolescent's life at any given time. Stress at home may contribute to them feeling irritable at school. Anxiety over a test may cause them to feel a lack of confidence. A fun interaction with a romantic interest might spark silliness or affection. The fact is, so much of a teen's behavior isn't directly related to the issue at hand, which can be hard for teens to remember when their peers act out (even though this is their reality, too).

Daughter: Meghan was so grouchy today in practice. She totally yelled at Lexie.
Parent: Do you know why?
Daughter: I don't know. Lexie didn't know either.
Parent: Is Meghan feeling stressed about something else? Maybe it didn't have anything to do with Lexie.
Daughter: Maybe. She did say she had tons of homework and she lost her cell phone because she got a D in math.
Parent: That's too bad. She sounds really overwhelmed.
Daughter: Probably. I hope Lexie doesn't stay mad at her.

Say This, Not That!

One of the toughest parts of unstable teen friendships is how relentless the social pressures are. No sooner is one friendship smoothed over than another incident makes waves. As adults, we recognize that this turmoil is a season in one's life; it's an aspect of growing that eventually fades as we learn how to set boundaries, communicate more effectively, and control our impulses. However, the inundation of technology means that kids rarely get a break. Texts, social media posts, and the immediate flow of gossip make it nearly impossible for kids to pause, reflect, and change their course of action or allow emotions to cool.

Your teen needs a voice of reason, your quiet confidence in them, and accessibility to your listening ear and discernment as to when an adult may need to get involved. It can be hard for teens to step back, consider the context, and reconsider their original assumptions. It's likely that your teen will need a lot of support with this. Here's some language to consider:

SAY THIS	NOT THAT
I'm sorry this is so tough for you. You're not alone in feeling this way.	This is just how teenagers are!
What do you have control of in this situation?	Just don't be friends with them.
This will get better.	Just wait a day or two; you'll get over this. Teenagers are just dramatic.
I want you to take a break from social media. What is something we can do instead?	Give me your phone. I'm tired of all this drama.

SOCIAL COMPARISON

Adolescents are extraordinarily self-focused. Their default thinking process is to consider themselves first, others next. While it might seem like this behavior is born of selfishness, it's actually a teen's response to learning that the greater world doesn't match up with their perception of how it's supposed to be. Teens start to recognize that adults don't know everything, rules are often arbitrary, and society is filled with pockets of hypocrisy and unfairness. Once adolescents gain awareness of these flaws, they often become more self-reflective, searching for their own inconsistencies and figurative blemishes. With this self-reflection inevitably comes the inaccurate belief that everyone is watching their every action. I distinctly recall my 13-year-old daughter cringing in embarrassment as we walked into a grocery store, certain that everyone would notice a smear of jelly on her sweatshirt. She kept her arms crossed over the offending spot and audibly breathed a sigh of relief when we reached the car. In reality, no one noticed or cared about her stained sweatshirt. But from her perspective, there might as well have been a neon sign on her forehead that announced, "Disgusting Girl Here!"

Why Do Adolescents Compare Themselves to Others?

During middle adolescence, self-concept, or the sense of who one is, is in its early stages. While your child may characterize themselves as an athlete, an artist, an academic, or all three, these categories may be fleeting, depending on factors such as parental support, acceptance of peers, cultural expectations, and the effort required to participate in the activities associated with this identity.

Related to self-concept is self-esteem, which includes a self-evaluation about whether one is good or bad as compared to others. As teens seek to understand themselves, they often do so in the context of comparing themselves to their peers. Am I an athlete if I'm not as good as Sam? Does this represent me based on how others view me? Will I be liked and accepted if I explore this more fully? Is everyone watching me as I try this new thing? Will I be laughed at?

How to Help Your Adolescent Cope with Social Comparison

Social comparison, while difficult for parents to observe, is a developmentally appropriate aspect of adolescence. Although it is relatively long-lived, sometimes lasting well into adulthood (we all know at least one adult whose self-esteem is based on how others view them), with appropriate support it will decrease in intensity over time.

1. **Validate your teen's feelings.** While it may be tempting to brush off their concerns as silly or dramatic, it's important to recognize the value of acknowledging

your teen's feelings. If they feel like you're going to disregard their perspective, they'll likely stop telling you their viewpoints and you'll lose the opportunity to stay connected and guide them toward more productive ways of thinking.

Daughter: I feel like everyone is staring at me because I have a big zit on my nose.
Parent: You're feeling self-conscious about it?
Daughter: Yeah. It's huge.
Parent: I know you feel that it's obvious, but it's not. I haven't seen anyone look at you in a way that suggests they've noticed it.

2. **Don't encourage irrational thinking.** Acknowledging your teen's feelings is not the same as validating those feelings or treating their perspective as though it's rational. It's unhelpful to get into an argument or debate, because that can cause teens to double down on their flawed thinking, but gently pointing out information that contradicts their statements is important in guiding them toward more accurate self-reflection.

Son: Everyone hates me. I have no friends.
Parent: What makes you feel like you have no friends?
Son: I don't know. I have no one to hang out with. Not one single person wants to spend time with me.
Parent: Jaylen came over yesterday and you two played basketball. And we carpooled with Malcolm on the way to school, and you were both laughing hysterically at something you were watching on your phone.
Son: Whatever. They don't even like me.

Parent: I disagree. And Mrs. Sherwood said that Jack always wants you to come over to swim in their pool with him. I understand that you may *feel* as though you haven't been connecting with friends lately, but I just want to remind you of all the kids you've really enjoyed spending time with over the last few days.

3. **Take advantage of opportunities to foster empathy.** When your teen expresses self-consciousness or self-doubt, remind them that their peers often feel that way, too. Encourage them to show compassion to others by saying something supportive, giving a compliment or reassurance, using humor, or doing something helpful. Recognizing that their peers experience these same feelings helps kids feel less isolated.

   Daughter: Ainsley dropped her drink today during lunch and the bottle broke. It made a huge mess.
   Parent: That's too bad. How did she react?
   Daughter: She was really embarrassed.
   Parent: Yeah, I'd probably feel that way, too. Did you help her clean it up?
   Daughter: No, I should have. That probably would have made her feel less embarrassed.
   Parent: Next time.

4. **Teach them how to use positive self-talk.** Often the most critical voice in our child's life is their own. Actively coach them to identify the negative things they say to themselves, like "I'm so awkward." Then, teach them to reframe these statements into something more accurate or positive, like "I'm feeling awkward because I'm standing here by myself, but I can handle this and it will be over soon." Sometimes kids benefit from a cheerful or silly mantra, like "I'm awesome,

amazing, and adorable." Encourage them to repeat it to themselves when they feel discouraging thoughts creep in. I've glanced at my son's phone and found texts he's written to himself with similar sentiments. He says he sometimes texts these types of statements to himself when he's standing at the bus stop with a group of kids he doesn't know. It gives him something to do and makes him feel better about himself.

Parent: **How are you feeling about today's history test?**
Teen: **A little nervous.**
Parent: **What kind of messages are you sending to yourself? What's your brain saying? Something kind or something negative?**
Teen: **It's telling me that the test might be too hard.**
Parent: **Maybe you could say to your brain, "This test might be hard, but I studied a lot and I can do well."**

The well-meaning parent, cringing at their discouraged teen's negative, largely untrue statements, just wants them to stop. They say things like "Why do you care about what Sarah thinks?" or "If all your friends were going to jump off a bridge, would you jump, too?" But in reality, adults send mixed messages to teens. In fact, we *do* want them to care about what other people think—namely, their parents and other trusted adults.

Adults regularly tell their teens their perspectives, and can feel really frustrated if teens don't see the situation in the same way or follow their directions. But adults also claim that they don't want teens to base their self-esteem on the view of their peers. Well, until adults want them to, that is—like when adults attempt to trigger self-awareness and desired social skills by saying, "Would you act like that in front of your friends? Wouldn't you be embarrassed if your friends knew you did that?" or "Is everyone else going to be dressed so casually at the dance?" or "Caroline is a soccer player. Wouldn't you like to be on the team with her?"

Say This, Not That!

Parents should work to send consistent messages to their teens about how to deal with social comparison, rather than expecting teens to decipher on their own when such comparison is appropriate and when it's counterproductive. Here are some statements that can help teens make sense of these confusing feelings:

SAY THIS	NOT THAT
I've felt that way, too.	You shouldn't feel that way. Stop saying that.
Thank you for telling me.	That's ridiculous.
How can I help?	I don't know what you want me to do about it.
I know you don't feel you're good at (insert skill or activity). Is it something you'd like to get better at, or is it just wishful thinking?	You're great at everything you do, honey!
Would you like to know my perspective, or would you rather I just listen?	You're overreacting. You just need to (insert action).

THE ROLE OF TECHNOLOGY AND SOCIAL MEDIA

The average age kids receive their first cell phone is 10 years old; by the beginning of high school, nearly 90 percent of teens have a cell phone with a data plan. Although kids have access to the Internet via computers, laptops, tablets, and gaming systems, smart phones have become the norm and, often, the tool they use to manage almost every part of their lives. Kids use smart phones to make calls, text, e-mail, make and watch videos, surf the Internet, live stream, play online games, and access social media accounts. Even middle school teachers increasingly assume that their students will have access to a smart phone and prompt them to download educational apps, take pictures of important materials, and access their e-mail and online grades at a moment's notice. Cell phones play a significant role in kids' development, but technological advances also make it difficult for parents to monitor their kids' usage and safety.

Why Is Technology So Important to Adolescents?

Given how important social connection is, it stands to reason that adolescents love having unlimited access to peers. With the flick of their thumbs, kids and teens can text, access images, take selfies, and send and receive videos. This allows them an outlet to express themselves, access information immediately, or feel part of a group even when they're home alone in their bedroom.

With this constant access comes pressure. Texts must be answered immediately, social outings that exclude a peer are quickly revealed, romantic interests are tracked via their "check-ins," and selfies require cute outfits and an all-encompassing knowledge of chin positioning. It's simultaneously exciting, awful, and utterly compelling.

How to Help Your Adolescent Navigate Technology

Kids need considerable support from adults in order to learn how to use technology in a safe and responsible way. While this book can't provide an in-depth review of all the strategies available to help parents educate their kids on appropriate technology usage, here are some general suggestions to consider:

1. **Be proactive, not reactive.** One of the most common missteps made by parents is their unwavering belief of "My kid is a nice kid and they know not to make poor choices." Yes, your kid is absolutely a nice kid, but they still have underdeveloped decision-making skills and little ability to see the big picture. So expecting them to restrain themselves when they're tempted to forward an inappropriate text, click on an inappropriate hashtag, or say something hateful online is unrealistic. Therefore, it's essential to know the common pitfalls kids experience online, discuss the risks, and brainstorm how to avoid them. Some topics to consider include safety from online predators, cyberbullying, and sexually inappropriate material, as well as safe social media behavior. Parents should not assume that their child knows better, and it should be stated clearly and repeatedly that technology is a privilege, it will only be used in collaboration with parents, and it will be permitted only to the degree to which kids have the maturity and ability to manage it.

2. **Create a written plan and review it regularly.** Writing down rules, expectations, and consequences increases the level of accountability felt by parents and kids. Be as specific as possible, avoiding vague phrases like "make good choices online." Most importantly, review the plan at regular intervals, at a minimum every three to six months (put a reminder in your calendar). All too often parents create a plan, tuck it in a drawer, and never revisit it. The plan needs to grow with your child, helping them gain competence and independence so they can self-monitor when they're older.

    Kid: I really want to get a certain gaming app.
    Parent: Is it one of the apps we said no to when we wrote our contract?

Kid: Yes, but you also said we could talk about it if I earned all As and Bs on my report card. Well, I did.
Parent: Okay. Let me look up some information about the app and we'll talk about it tomorrow.

3. **Remember the good things.** It's important to remember that although using technology is a serious responsibility, there are also benefits. Most schoolwork and academic information can be accessed online, whether it's via a teacher's website, Google Classroom, or websites related to a particular topic. Texting, social media, and gaming are the primary ways that adolescents communicate, and they often use them to communicate positive things like encouraging words, compliments, and humor. Your prickly preteen may be more communicative when a parent sends a prompt in the form of a friendly text or a silly Snapchat, or shows their skill at referencing a popular meme.

Parent: (texts kid a GIF that shows a kid sweeping)
Kid: (texts back a GIF of a kid rolling his eyes and saying, "Okay, Dad.")

4. **Use technology to monitor technology.** Parents often believe that they can adequately monitor their child's technology usage via "spot checks" and arbitrary time restrictions. In reality, your child's ability to skirt boundaries established by parents and website user agreements far surpasses that of adults; after all, adults don't have to be crafty in order to have unrestricted access to the Internet. Parents should take advantage of the wide range of tools available. Tools may include parental controls that restrict access to explicit material and undesirable apps, apps that monitor content and alert parents of troublesome

Internet searches and content, and apps that restrict inappropriate content. While these tools aren't perfect and don't replace an attentive parent, they can discourage a child from making impulsive decisions with their phone.

Parent: **Kiddo, I have this new app. It keeps me up-to-date on your search history and topics you're curious about.**
Kid: **Am I going to get in trouble if I search something you don't want me to?**
Parent: **No, it's more about me knowing that you have questions about something. Then we can set aside some time to talk about it.**

5. **Monitor, don't spy.** Kids benefit from being fully aware that parents are attentive to their technology usage. They make better decisions and are more likely to communicate a concern or stressor to an adult. Be transparent about the fact that you're planning to stay abreast of current online trends, will access your kid's phone regularly, and will provide them with increased amounts of privacy as they demonstrate they can handle the privilege of using technology.

Parent: **Did you know that kids are less likely to send and receive naked pictures if they know that their parent MIGHT look at their phone?**
Kid (shudders): **OMG, it would be *horrible* if you or Dad saw a naked picture of one of my friends.**
Parent: **How would you feel if one of your friends' parents saw a naked picture of *you*?**
Kid: **NIGHTMARE.**
Parent: **Seriously. Makes you think twice, doesn't it?**

Say This, Not That!

All kids and teens make mistakes with technology at some point. Hopefully, their mistakes won't be too costly; it only takes a moment for a social media post to go awry. Kids need to know that although they're expected to use common sense and follow established rules at all times, parents are a good resource for help and guidance when missteps occur. Here's some wording that might be helpful when the time comes:

SAY THIS	NOT THAT
You're going to make mistakes. I don't expect you to be perfect.	We've talked about this over and over. Why don't you get it?
If you don't follow the rules, you will lose the privilege of using your phone.	Give me that. I can't stand looking at you playing on your phone for another minute.
I see that your friend posted something on social media that wasn't appropriate. Let's talk about her choice.	Block that person. They're clearly bad news.
I'm going to be keeping an eye on what you do online. It's really hard for a kid to manage it by themselves.	You'd better not do something stupid online or you'll lose your phone until you're 16.

SKILL DEVELOPMENT AND RESPONSIBILITIES

The transition from elementary to middle school can be a major whirlwind for kids. Their bodies are changing, socialization takes priority, and the level of responsibility they're expected to display increases significantly. Even though they may have started to look more like adults, most teens struggle to consistently manage these expectations on a daily basis. Into this whirlwind step parents, whose goal is to help shelter their teen from the storm by providing them with support, encouraging them to practice new skills, helping them learn to deal with disappointment, and teaching them how to ask for help when they most need it.

What Skills Should Parents Prioritize?

I often work with parents who feel overwhelmed by the lack of urgency their teens display when it comes to their responsibilities. They'll use statements like "She doesn't care about her grades," "He has no interest in personal hygiene," "Her room is a disaster," "He wastes time and doesn't ever get to bed before midnight." They feel as if their teen's life is a bit of a mess and don't know how hard to press them. Should they withhold privileges? Let natural consequences occur? Lecture? Reinforce the good and ignore the missteps? Parents often use all these strategies but apply them inconsistently, which can make them frustrated. Instead, use these questions to figure out which skills you should be focused on:

1. **Is this task essential to adult life?** If the task is not directly related to your teen's ability to function as a young adult, then it might be helpful to consider whether the power struggle is worth it. For example, one can be a productive adult even if they fail to make their bed, wear clothes that have been lying on the floor instead of hung neatly in the closet, and eat carb-laden breakfasts. In contrast, they cannot be a productive adult if they fail high school, have no idea how to save money, never arrive to work on time, regularly fail to get enough sleep, and don't know how to set boundaries in their relationships. Therefore, focus on these big-picture things. Spend time

giving direct instruction in how to do these things, reinforcing them when they do them well, and helping them when they struggle.

2. **Are you helping or hurting their growth?** This is a doozy. Often parents feel like they're helping or being supportive when they manage tasks for their child. They may create a study guide for their child (without the child's help), pack up their backpack each morning, fill out job applications for them, clean their room, e-mail a teacher to ask a question, schedule social plans with peers, etc. While well intentioned, being overly involved can result in a child feeling helpless and overwhelmed on the rare occasion when they have to step up. This inhibits their motivation to initiate tasks and to persist when confronted with failure, increasing their dependency on the parent.

How to Help Your Adolescent as They Develop Responsibilities

1. **Clearly define which skills you expect them to work on.** Rather than peppering your teen throughout the day with a series of directives in the form of verbal instructions, reminder texts, exasperated sighs, and lectures about where they're falling short, pick one or two areas that need improvement. Some examples include getting up on time, getting ready in the morning, leaving on time for school, establishing age-appropriate bedtime routines, or getting homework and studying done on their own. The focus should be on defining the behavior that you'd like to see, rather than creating a laundry list of all the times they've failed at exhibiting this behavior.

Parent: Hey, bud. Let's figure out a plan for school mornings.
Teen: Huh? What do you mean?
Parent: I feel like I'm doing a lot of yelling and nagging in the morning to get you up and out the door on time for school.
Teen: Yeah, that sucks.
Parent: Now that you're in middle school, I want you to be able to get up on your own.

2. **Focus on specific strategies that can be used to develop the desired skill.** When communicating with your teen about the preferred skill you'd like them to develop, it's important to focus on the specific strategies and routines that will be used and modified, rather than having an extensive conversation about why your child needs to agree with your opinion about how essential this skill is. Pointing out how horrible and nonproductive their life will be if they don't learn a skill imminently is neither helpful nor going to elicit their buy-in. State your expectation, then initiate a collaborative conversation to make an action plan.

Parent: I was thinking that instead of me nagging you in the morning, we could figure out some strategies to help you wake up without my help. I know your body just wants to keep sleeping in the morning.
Teen: I feel like I can't even open my eyes, and it's so annoying when you yell at me.
Parent: How about we start with using an alarm clock? Maybe turn the sound up and set it a few feet away so you have to get out of bed to turn it off.
Teen: That sounds awful.
Parent: It does. But I can't imagine me yelling at you sounds much better.

Teen: **Yeah, I guess. Can we turn it to the music setting instead of the buzzing sound?**
Parent: **We can try that for a few days. But if you still ignore it, we may have to switch it to the buzzing.**

From there, you can brainstorm about the type of alarm clock; come up with alternate strategies, like sleeping with the blinds open so natural light will help your teen wake up; negotiate a reasonable time for lights out the night before; have breakfast items available that can be eaten on the walk to the bus stop; agree that if they miss the bus and a parent has to drive them, they will pay for the gas used; etc.

3. **Decide on what role the parent should play to help support their teen.** In this example, the parent may agree to purchase the alarm clock, keep the pantry stocked with convenient breakfast items, and give one verbal warning 10 minutes prior to the time the bus is scheduled to arrive. The remainder of the tasks will be completed by the teen. Teens have much more investment in a plan that doesn't put all the responsibilities on them right away. As the child increases in independence, parents can phase themselves out of the plan or extend the plan to include a new challenge.

4. **Determine the consequences if the teen (or the parent) doesn't uphold their end of the agreement.** For example, if the teen fails to set the alarm prior to going to bed, he may lose the privilege of playing video games after school. If he gets up with the alarm but still doesn't complete his morning tasks in a timely manner, then the alarm will be adjusted to go off 10 minutes earlier the following day. You may be able to create a suitable plan together, but if there is no consequence to

disregarding it, then apathetic teens may prefer to rely on dear old Mom and Dad to get the task done.

Say This, Not That!

When teens aren't attending to their responsibilities—especially responsibilities that we consider to be standard and well within their skill set—we can feel frustrated, angry, and disrespected. Parents tend to cycle between being micromanagers who keep tabs on each step their teen makes and insisting each action be done to their standards, or throwing up their hands and saying, "Fine! You do it! Sink or swim." In reality, parents need to set an expectation, set the stage for success, and be available to reinforce or reteach when necessary. Here are a few statements that can help make that clear:

SAY THIS	NOT THAT
Let's work together to figure out this problem.	What's wrong with you?
Do you need help with this?	Why can't you do this?
You can do this, but it will take practice.	You shouldn't be acting like this at your age.
I think you'll feel proud of yourself once you start taking care of this on your own.	I'm disappointed in you.

Limit or Let Go

How do we give kids more freedom while still offering structure and guidance through this stage of adolescence? Here are a few ideas:

LIMIT	LET GO
Access to the Internet after a predetermined time of the night	Procrastination (if it's more annoying than detrimental)
Privileges and distractions when a grade is unacceptable due to a lack of effort	The occasional poor grade or missing assignment
Constant complaining or negativity	Venting about a social mishap for a limited period of time

Teen (laughs at a risqué joke while we're watching TV together)

Me (thinking): **Wait, how does she even know what that joke means? We've never even talked about that!**

Chapter Four

Late Adolescence:
The World According to Sex
(Ages 15-ish to 18-ish)

LATE ADOLESCENCE, WHICH TYPICALLY FALLS between the ages of 15 and 18-ish, is primarily experienced during the high school years. Parents often say that this period is defined by a constant push-pull, as adolescents think they know everything (but don't), need to experience independence (but make a lot of mistakes), and frequently enter into romantic partnerships that feel very grown up (but aren't emotionally mature just yet). The role of parents during this stage of life can vary. Some teens sail into late adolescence with a well-developed work ethic, a sense of competency, and well-defined personal goals. They seem to require little monitoring beyond being urged to get enough sleep and hang out with their families once in a while. For these teens, parents mainly serve as a support system in navigating logistics like applying for college financial aid, learning about birth control, and getting car repairs. Other teens struggle to develop the life skills parents deem necessary for adulthood. These teens may have trouble with grades, getting and keeping a job, developing a healthy social group, and managing routines independently. These struggles can contribute to a fractured parent-child relationship, as the teen's need for parental advice is likely high, but the interest in hearing it is nil. It can be hard for parents to recognize that this is a season of development that is likely to blow over in time, because while it's happening, it can be *very* stressful and anxiety-provoking for both parent and teen.

By this point, much of the teen's life is lived outside of their parents' home, as school, work, socialization, and extracurricular activities all tend to take precedence over dear ol' Mom and Dad. Best-case scenario, communication might be warm but infrequent; worst-case scenario, you may feel like you're involved in a high-stakes business negotiation every time you ask your kid how their day was. Now the most physically transformative stages of puberty are over, and teens' bodies resemble those of adults. Milestones such as driver's licenses, after-school jobs, modified class schedules, and dating privileges make a teen's life more closely resemble an adult's life. Youths in this age group are constantly asked, "What do you want to do after high school?" or "What career are you interested in?" Both parents and teens are aware of their looming future and may engage in constant comparison with same-age peers about college prospects, athletic ability, job skills, travel, or living arrangements.

What's Going On? Characteristics Associated with Late Adolescence

PHYSICALLY

By this point, thankfully, puberty is in the rearview mirror of most teens, though acne and overactive sweat glands may still be a daily battle, especially for boys. The defining aspect of this stage is no longer changing bodies; now it's thinking about how to use them.

At this age, sexuality is a defining aspect of identity. Adolescents may be asking themselves questions like "Who am I attracted to?," "What am I ready for?," "How do my feelings interact with my family's values?," "How connected do I feel to others?," "How connected do I need to feel in order to have sex with someone?" They'll also be thinking about sex, talking about sex, reading about sex, watching sex (real and simulated) online and in films, and very possibly experimenting with sex. Today's teens know much more about sex than their parents did at their age, and have access to a seemingly infinite number of information sources—some accurate, some less so. They can easily view porn, will hear varying opinions about whether monogamy is necessary in a sexual relationship, and will be surrounded by rampant sexting.

Dealing with all of this might make some parents long for the nice, soothing power struggles of middle adolescence. But parents of late adolescents have a decision to make. They can either dive right into the discussion, or put their hands over their ears and sing "la-la-la-la-la." Only you can decide how to approach talking to your teen about sexuality, though research tells us that discussing sex with teens in an open and nonshaming way is strongly correlated with healthy sexual development.

EMOTIONALLY

With all the heightened awareness of sex, the desire to make their own choices, and the slow realization that decisions made today have an impact on tomorrow, most late adolescents are experiencing significant emotional upheaval. The pressure to perform, whether academically, athletically, or within a relationship, can induce equal amounts of anxiety and confidence. During this stage of life, teens often actively explore the options that parents have mindfully steered them away from, which can mean experimenting with drug and alcohol use, entering a relationship with a person of a significantly different background, moving toward or away from a specific religious belief system, or considering post–high school educational or job choices that differ from what their parents would prefer. Teens at this age can act defensively, withhold information because they think a parent will lecture or judge, or impulsively make a choice without stopping to think or consult someone more experienced. They're walking the line between doing what feels right for them and worrying about disappointing others, and this can cause a significant amount of angst.

SOCIALLY

During the later teen years, friendships still ebb and flow as teens explore various parts of their identities. The friendships that do endure are based on a sense of connection, shared experiences, and a belief that the relationship is caring, consistent, and enjoyable. Teens often struggle to decipher the difference between relationships that contain healthy amounts of turmoil and those that are toxic. This can be extraordinarily stressful for parents, especially if they see their child dating a controlling partner, becoming the victim of peer pressure, or struggling with peers who alternately accept and reject them.

Brain Change

During late adolescence, the brain is approximately 80 percent of the way to maturity. But the frontal lobe, responsible for planning and self-control, is the slowest part of the brain to develop, and thus still a work in progress. Its underdevelopment contributes greatly toward some of the most perplexing aspects of adolescence—for example, the mood swings, the impulsivity, and the temptation to engage in risky behavior. In addition, the teen brain has a constant desire for reward, triggered by an increase in the activity of the neural circuits that release dopamine—a neurotransmitter responsible for that rush we feel while doing something exciting. This means that teens naturally struggle to put on the brakes while something feels good (or has the potential to feel good), whether it's putting down the video game controller, dragging themselves out of bed in the morning, or stopping to think about birth control during an intimate moment with a partner.

What to Expect

Adolescents in this age range strongly gravitate toward their peers rather than their parents. At times, it seems as if they're living a life entirely separate from the one their parents have cultivated with them for the past 15 or 16 years. They're part of communities that parents may not have a role in, such as those at their after-school job, within their social media platforms, or within an extra-curricular activity. Recently, one of my teen clients said he feels emotionally closest to members of an online support group for gay and lesbian youth. He felt they knew his innermost thoughts and were consistently supportive of his goal to become an artist. Their interactions felt free of "real life" pressure to look and act a certain way. His parents had no knowledge of his membership in this group. Why not? "I don't know," he said. "I don't think they'd mind. They know I'm gay. They'd probably feel better knowing that my friends are so good to me. But it just feels like my space and I don't really want it to be interrupted by their constant questions." Other teens report that it feels like their parents are always worrying—for example, if they'll get hurt, if they're planning for their future, if they're getting everything done, etc. It feels easier to withdraw from the adults in their lives, stumble through as best they can, and ask for help later if necessary.

RISKY BEHAVIOR

During late adolescence, teens are gripped by the urge to experiment. Although this period of experimentation may extend well into their mid 20s, teens in late adolescence face the highest risk of being harmed while experimenting because they have little skill or desire to engage in judicious decision making. This is paired with a dangerous belief of "it won't happen to me." Sure, teens in this age group have heard the horror stories: the classmate who drowned after swimming while intoxicated, the teen from a rival high school who died in a motorcycle accident, the friend of a friend of a friend who fell off a cliff while taking a selfie. But often, these stories don't have much of an impact, especially considering that for every tragedy tied to poor teen decision making, there are hundreds of harrowing stories that ended with no more than a headache and punishment from an angry parent. The urge toward risky behavior, combined with a lack of forethought and a sense of invincibility, can be scary, leading parents to waver between conviction that their teen "knows better" and fretting about potential worst-case scenarios.

Why Do Teens Engage in Risky Behavior?

Teens are at a time of life when they have many of the freedoms of an adult—a driver's license, less supervision, and access to money, for example—but lack the maturity to consistently make responsible decisions. That drive to trigger a dopamine release is real, and without it, teens can feel bored, restless, and impatient. As a result, there is a constant search for stimulation. The majority of the time, teens satisfy this need with video games, physical activity, carbohydrates, social media, and social interaction in general. But sometimes, teens also feel the urge to really amplify the rush. Imagine a Friday night with absent parents, access to alcohol, some lively music, and an audience of same-age peers. While it's a night likely to result in moderate alcoholic excess and some very unflattering pictures posted on social media, it could also end in regret or serious harm. Why are teens so likely to participate in risky behavior?

1. **Teens are hyperrational.** One myth about teens is that they don't know how dangerous their behavior is, that they just don't understand the risks. But actually, they *do* know the risks. However, teens tend toward hyperrationality, a term coined by Dr. Daniel Siegel, which refers to the fact that teens tend to focus less on the risks and more on the benefits. They have more information than any previous generation about the dangers of risky behavior. Social media spreads stories about every one-in-a-million tragedy far and wide, parents tell their own stories about dangerous behavior, and schools make a concerted effort to educate kids on the risks associated with activities like substance use, unprotected sex, and texting and driving. But even with all that information, the payoff seems too great. So instead of asking, "Why do this?" teens ask, "Why not?" And to their teen brain the "why not" is never as awesome as the "why."

2. **Teens are greatly influenced by their friends.** Decision making changes even more when teens have a peer to reinforce their already skewed thinking. Consider the more titillating (or shameful) stories from your own youth. They didn't occur while you were home alone in your room, doing algebra proofs. They occurred while you were with at least one other person, most likely a friend around your age, and had some other risk factor present, such as alcohol, a lack of supervision, or simply an urge to relieve boredom. When these conditions are in place, the cautionary words of Mom and Dad fade, replaced by a huge light-up sign in the teen brain that reads, "Good feelings, this way!"

The resulting actions may look like impulsivity, but they're actually the result of a tendency to suspend the sense of foreboding and clear a path toward action. And given that teens now have 24-hour access to peers via social media, as well as the ability to live stream, peer influence is relentless.

How to Help Your Teen Make Safer Choices

Knowing that your teen is going out to explore the world and will inevitably engage in risky or downright dangerous behavior is stressful. Even just standing by while they drive a car to school or walk through a dark parking lot after a shift at work can make it hard for us to take a deep breath. But then there are the times when your teen will actively try out a genuinely risky behavior, such as smoking marijuana, experimenting with sexual activity, or going to a party at the house of someone they've never met. You might feel helpless and filled with dread as you watch them text furiously to make plans on a Friday night, get ready to go to prom, or come in the house smelling like smoke. But even if you're struggling with an overwhelming feeling of dread, there are ways to help encourage your teen to make good choices.

1. **Recognize that this is a legitimate part of development.** Even though parents would love to get a time machine and transport themselves past these years of impulsivity and novelty seeking (ideally landing in a time when their child is a mature adult who doesn't constantly ask for gas money), it's important to understand that this stage is essential to overall development. Teens need to undergo the process of pushing away their parents, making mistakes, and trying new things. It allows them to test the limits of their skills, make adjustments, and practice adulting, all while they're within arm's reach of a responsible adult. During this time, teens have heightened emotional states and gravitate toward social connectedness that will serve them well as they leave

the nest. While you probably won't be able to fully embrace this stage no matter how much you read about it, you should at least acknowledge that this stage is a means to an end. In the meantime, you can remind teens of safety rules and expectations. You can also focus on taking care of yourself during these high-stress situations: Get enough sleep, vent, get reassurance from friends or a co-parent, and take time to explore your own interests—anything besides counting the minutes until curfew.

Parent: **You look cute. Where are you going?**
Teen: **To a party at Aiden's house.**
Parent: **Tell me what you're going to do to stay safe.**
Teen (sighing): **I'll stay with at least one friend at all times, I won't drink enough to impair my judgment, and I'll take an Uber home with a friend. Jess is going to ride home with me and she'll spend the night here. Also, my phone is charged and I have my debit card.**
Parent: **And you know you can call me if you need anything? No matter how late?**

2. **Encourage self-reflection.** In my former life as a school psychologist, our team of educators often examined kids' misbehavior by asking the question "What need is this child trying to meet?" The answer might include the need for attention, control, stimulation, or social connection, or the need to avoid fear or embarrassment. Once our team was able to figure out the child's need, we'd find ways for them to meet it in a socially appropriate way. In my counseling work, I often ask teens to consider the needs they attempt to meet on a regular basis. Often, teens express that they want to earn attention from a parent or a romantic interest. Others indicate that they feel that

life is just "too much" sometimes, their emotions are just too intense, and they just want to distract themselves from that pressure. Others are quickly bored and restless and are looking for stimulation. But I've learned that teaching a teen how to be mindful and self-reflective and to identify their emotions is essential to them being able to choose to meet their needs in a prosocial way.

Parent: **Dude, check in with yourself.**
Teen: **What do you mean?**
Parent: **You seem like you've got a lot of nervous energy. And you keep checking your phone. What's up?**
Teen: **I texted some people because I want to see if anyone's going to get together tonight, and no one's answered.**
Parent: **So you're feeling lonely and trying to find someone to talk to? Or are you trying to find something to do that's fun?**
Teen: **I've been cooped up in school all week. I want to go play soccer or run around the lake. I feel like I'm going crazy just sitting around.**

In this scenario, it would be easy for a parent to make assumptions about why their teen was so restless. It wouldn't have taken much for that teen to express frustration or impatience and lash out in an attempt to meet their need for physical interaction. Instead, the parent encourages the teen to "check in" with themselves and stop and think about what need they may be trying to meet. If the scenario were to continue, it might progress to the parent helping their teen sort out the most realistic way to get that need met.

Teach Your Teen to Make Decisions

Now, notice I didn't say "help them make decisions." It's more about teaching them strategies when it comes to decision making.

1. **Reinforce the idea that they have control over the decisions they make, even if it can be hard to recall that in the heat of the moment.** Parents can coach teens to tell a peer, "Hang on. Let me think for a minute," or to take five deep breaths before doing something they may regret. Practice doing this in front of them and with them.

2. **Reinforce the idea that NOT making a decision is, in fact, a form of making a decision.** If someone is trying to decide whom to ask to prom, but time goes by and they don't decide, soon it's too late to ask anyone. By not deciding whom to take, they have actually decided to go alone or not to go at all. That same cause-and-effect can apply to numerous situations in their lives.

3. **Learn to use intuition.** The teenage brain gravitates toward hyperrational thinking, which influences teens to give the pros more weight than the cons. That's why it's important to link decisions to the more intuitive portion of the mind—that is, the part that responds when asked, "Does this feel right? Is this actually going to get me something I want or need? Is this worth getting in trouble or potentially getting hurt?" When teens link their decisions to the more self-reflective part of their brain, rather than the "go do things that feel good" part of the brain, better decisions result.

   Teen 1: **Let's go drive the car on Lake Road. We can time each other to see how fast we go between the park and the lake.**
   Teen 2: **That road is very windy. It's dark, man.**

Teen 1: I know. It will be awesome. Last week Dev and I did it, and he did it in six minutes and I did it in five and a half. I'm going to try to beat my time.
Teen 2: Seriously, man. I'm not doing that. Let's go play basketball at the park. I'll drive.

Say This, Not That!

The stress of parenting during adolescence—a time when teens' brains are actively urging them toward exciting but potentially unsafe activities—is fierce. It's hard not to take it personally when your teen doesn't seem to care about your worries, let alone make choices based on them. While not every teen is a risk taker, nearly all of them step outside their comfort zones at times. Parents must keep the lines of communication open, gently and persistently remind their teen of safety measures and decision-making power, and remember that in a few short years, this stage will pass. Here are some statements that parents can make during those moments when the teen brain seems to be taking over:

SAY THIS	NOT THAT
Are you feeling overwhelmed?	You're acting crazy.
Let's talk about some things to consider before you make this decision.	Because I said no.
This is a situation where you're being asked to make an adult decision with a teenage brain.	You think you know everything, but you don't.
Let's both take a deep breath. We don't need to decide this right this minute.	Fine. Just do what you want, but don't come crying to me.

DEVELOPING BOUNDARIES

One of the most challenging parts of learning how to interact with others is understanding and establishing boundaries. Loosely defined, boundaries are limits, or guidelines, that one uses to ensure that others treat them safely and with respect. Everyone should have boundaries; we are tasked with establishing and upholding our own, plus recognizing and respecting the boundaries of others. Part of boundary setting is identifying how you will respond if someone violates your boundaries.

Because a teen's overarching goals are fitting in, being accepted by their peers, and feeling included, establishing boundaries is very difficult. It requires teens to do a lot of self-examination, which may be difficult considering their brains are not yet fully developed. It also requires that teens assert themselves in a manner that may contradict a peer's (and sometimes an adult's) intent and cause them to suffer the consequences, which could be considerable. But setting boundaries, while difficult at first, will pay off immensely. Not just because teens will likely feel empowered and more in control after setting them, but because boundaries make it more likely that their peers will treat them better, too.

Why Adolescents Need to Develop Appropriate Boundaries

1. **To keep them physically safe.** Teens with physical boundaries understand their need for physical space, privacy, and control over their bodies. Do they know how to avoid an unwanted hug? How to say no to getting into a car with someone who has been drinking? Whether or not they feel safe when left home alone at night or are asked to watch a horror movie?

2. **To keep them sexually safe.** This is a tough one, but it's intermingled with sexual desire, wanting to be appreciated by a love interest, cultural or parental expectations, and comfort level with sexual touch and activity (what, where, when, and with whom). It can also be linked to asserting oneself when it comes to using contraceptives.

3. **To keep them emotionally safe.** A concept that I often teach my young clients is "You're not responsible for someone else's emotions." And conversely, "They're not responsible for your emotions." Understanding these concepts can protect teens from blaming others, accepting unwarranted blame, feeling guilty for someone else's negative feelings, becoming overly dependent on someone's view of them, being emotionally manipulated, and feeling overly sensitive to the comments of others.

Why Do Adolescents Struggle with Setting Boundaries?

The primary reason adolescents struggle with setting boundaries is because they aren't taught how to do so. Boundary setting is learned, and it usually takes direct instruction by a parent or caregiver over a long period of time to teach children and teens how to set boundaries.

Here is a list of other reasons adolescents struggle to create healthy boundaries:

1. **Being afraid of disappointing someone.** Despite this developmental stage being a time of relative self-absorption, it can be difficult for teens to put their own needs ahead of a friend's. If I tell my BFF that she can't borrow my laptop after she was grounded from using hers, will she be mad at me?

2. **Feeling as if they don't have the power or control to set boundaries.** If your teen has always been taught that they must obey adult directions, then they will feel incapable of asserting their boundaries for fear of getting in trouble. How can your teen tell the youth group leader that she feels uncomfortable when he asks her to organize the supply closet with him while no one else is around?

3. **Being afraid of looking stupid or being embarrassed.** The urge to look calm or "cool" is intense in this age group. If I tell my date that I'm not interested in having sex with him, will he call me a baby? If I reveal to my friend that her behavior hurt me, will my vulnerability make me look stupid?

4. **They don't know what feels right yet.** Boundaries transform as we age and enter new developmental stages, and it can be difficult to know yourself well enough to set clear ones. In addition, what feels good one day might feel uncomfortable the next.

How Do We Help Late Adolescents Establish Healthy Boundaries?

1. **Role model healthy boundaries.** This is essential. If your child sees you saying no to the request to join a school committee because your work schedule is hectic, firmly telling a stranger to give you more space in the grocery store line, telling their sibling to stop interrupting them in the bathroom, or telling your mother to stop giving unsolicited marriage advice, then you're role modeling boundaries. It can also be helpful to discuss times when you've struggled to set boundaries ("I didn't know how to tell your grandmother that I didn't want her in the room when I was giving birth, and now every picture from that

moment has her in it"). Television shows, news stories, and even celebrity gossip can include powerful examples of boundary setting, and they can be discussed in a casual way without making the teen feel pressured. Making these discussions part of everyday life can be very helpful.

Daughter: **Andrew asked Grace to the dance.**
Parent: **Is she going to go with him?**
Daughter: **She doesn't want to, but they're good friends and she doesn't want to hurt his feelings. He really likes her and wants to be her boyfriend.**
Parent: **Do you think she should be someone's date if she doesn't want to go with him?**
Daughter: **No, probably not. I think she needs to tell him nicely that she doesn't want to go.**
Parent: **That sounds like a good idea. She can be kind and still set a boundary about whether their relationship is going to be boyfriend and girlfriend.**

2. **Teach them how to impose consequences if their boundaries aren't respected.** This may mean pushing through an uncomfortable moment to make sure they adhere to their self-imposed values or limitations.

Parent: **You going out tonight with Thomas?**
Son: **No, I'm pissed at him.**
Parent: **What happened?**
Son: **I told him about something Madeline told me, and he said something to her about it.**
Parent: **So you told him something in confidence about your girlfriend?**
Son: **Yeah. I thought I could trust him, but I was wrong.**
Parent: **So now what?**

Son: I'm angry, and when I calm down, I'm going to let him know that I don't trust him. And I'm going to be more careful about what I say around him.

Parent: How are things with Madeline?

Son: She's still upset, but at least she let me explain. We'll be okay. I definitely learned my lesson.

3. **Teach them about consent.** In general terms, consent means "to give permission." This might include a teen giving a friend permission to look up something on their phone, borrow some money, or enter their home. Consent in more specific terms includes voluntary permission to engage in sexual activity. Voluntary permission means that the person giving consent is giving it willingly (without coercion) and consciously (without being impaired by drugs, alcohol, unconsciousness, or sleep). In addition, consent cannot be given if there is a discrepancy in power between the two parties (such as one person being an authority figure).

Ideally, the concept of consent should be taught from an early age, starting in preschool and beyond. It should also be taught from the perspectives of both giving and receiving consent. Often, girls are taught about giving consent while boys are taught about receiving consent, but both girls and boys will be confronted with both types of situations.

In the home environment, it's essential to respect physical boundaries. One sister wants to have a sleepover, but the other sister wants her bed to herself? That needs to be respected; everyone can sleep in their own beds. One kid doesn't want to be tossed into the pool against their will? Then don't do it. One child doesn't want Mom to pick at their clothes or hair while they're heading out to a fancy event?

Mom can tell the child about the lint on her dress instead of poking at her. Kids need to be given permission to say no. They need to be listened to when they say no. Discuss it openly. Give them some suggestions of specific words they can use. Role-play it well before you think it will become necessary.

Teen: Ugh, I hate study hall.
Parent: Yeah? How come?
Teen: Tyler always wants to sit right next to me. He'll squish into the desk right next to mine and sit way too close to me, even though there are always plenty of empty desks.
Parent: That's not okay. Let's think of how you can respond so you don't have to sit with him. Have you told him you don't want him to sit so close to you?
Teen: I mainly just sigh loudly and roll my eyes.
Parent: How about, "Tyler. Sit over there so we're not all squished."
Teen: I think I can put my backpack on the seat of the desk next to me, too. So there's even less space.
Parent: Good idea. I do think you should also tell him how you feel. Be direct. It's okay to not want someone sitting too close to you. He should respect that.

Say This, Not That!

Teaching kids about boundaries can feel tricky, especially if your child is worried about peers understanding their limits. It can also be tough if you're worried that it will make your kids appear disrespectful, or if you struggle with establishing boundaries for yourself. But it's important to role model for teens that boundaries can be thoughtful, respectful, and still effective. Here are some ways to help your teen make their boundaries clear:

SAY THIS	NOT THAT
If she says she doesn't want to date you/kiss you/spend time with you, respect that and leave her alone.	Try again. Maybe she'll change her mind if you ask her again.
If you're not sure if it feels right, text me and I will come pick you up right away.	If someone asks you to do something, you could just try it once.
Let's think of some phrases you can use to say no in that situation. Then let's think of some things you can do if your friends aren't listening when you say no.	Just say no (without further explanation).
You're not responsible for their feelings. Be kind but maintain your boundaries.	But you might hurt their feelings.

SEX, SEX, SEX, SEX . . . OH, AND ROMANTIC PARTNERSHIPS

Some people experience the first flutters of sexual desire and curiosity as early as 10 years old. But as androgens and estrogens begin to be produced during puberty, those flutters turn into a strong desire to experience sexual release with a partner, and interacting with a crush becomes one of the most reliable sources of the dopamine late adolescents crave.

Most parents would prefer that teens wait until they're sufficiently mature and well adjusted to understand the physical, emotional, and social ramifications of sex (and for some, that means waiting until marriage). But the reality is that the average age for first intercourse is just shy of 18 years old, with about 13 percent of teens having first intercourse by age 15. Sexual experiences among teens are greatly influenced by social context, of course; studies have shown that teens are more likely to have sex at earlier ages when they have an earlier onset of puberty, are from a lower socioeconomic background, have a more impulsive personality, have lower self-esteem, and have friends who are sexually active. But research indicates that about 70 percent of high school seniors, across various backgrounds, believe that it's okay for teens to have sex. So it's essential for teens to be informed, to feel safe enough to ask questions, and to feel emotionally supported when it comes to sexual behavior.

Why Is It So Important for Parents to Communicate with Their Teens About Sex?

Sexual attitudes in North America are relatively restrictive. Typically, parents provide little to no information about sex and rarely talk about sex in the presence of their children. This is very contradictory to the messages spread within the media, where sexually focused television shows, music, social media, and Internet porn are prolific and easily accessible. Peers also aren't shy about talking about sex, and their conversations are often riddled with inaccuracies, gossip, and judgment. Your child's exposure to high-quality sex education in a school setting can vary greatly depending on the state, community, or school. Although conversations about the physical aspects of sex should take place at the cusp of puberty, these conversations need to extend to discussions about the emotional and social consequences of sexual behavior, as well as sensitive topics such as consent, sexual assault, sex trafficking, pregnancy, miscarriage, abortion, and laws and social policies. It's essential that parents take a leadership role in educating their children about sex, and these conversations should begin long before hormones take hold and influence decision making.

It's important to recognize that while sexual relationships are an inevitable part of reaching physical and emotional maturity, how teens approach this stage of development is greatly influenced by their family relationships. While peer groups socialize teens to become adults, the lessons they learn from parents and their family of origin transfer to these peer relationships. Here are some factors to consider:

1. **Body acceptance:** Children and teens are inundated with media and peer messages about bodies. Fashion, beauty products, pornography, social media influencers, and celebrities send overt or implicit messages to youth about standards of beauty. However, how parents communicate about their own bodies and those of their children is highly related to whether children value their own bodies. If teens are taught that their body is somehow inferior, then they are less likely to respect it by keeping it safe and advocating for themselves when they are in uncomfortable situations. Teens who feel their bodies are valuable and accepted will demand more respect from sexual partners.

2. **Self-esteem:** Whether we value ourselves is strongly related to how we interact with others. If we believe we're worthy of respect and feel our perspective should be valued, we're likely to develop relationships that support these values. We're likely to advocate for ourselves, challenge or reject others who we feel mistreat us, and show the ability to bounce back when we experience rejection. Positive self-esteem will equip teens with the mind-set to choose sexual partners who are healthy and loving.

3. **Knowledge:** It's much easier to make healthy decisions about sex when you're armed with accurate information. What's the difference between sexual behavior and sexual intercourse? Under what conditions can a teen get pregnant or acquire a sexually transmitted infection? What information should teens share with their doctor to ensure that they remain safe and healthy? What are the pros and cons of specific types of birth control? What should you do if you feel mistreated in a sexual interaction? How can you prevent a partner from feeling mistreated during a sexual interaction? How teens answer these questions will shape their sexual identities, and your teen is at less risk for a negative sexual experience if they're able to make informed, proactive choices.

How to Help Your Teen Make Healthy Choices About Sex

Parents have a wonderful opportunity to support and guide their teens as they evolve into sexual beings. In order to provide that support and guidance, however, a foundation must be built between teens and parents that is open and informative, and persists through the awkward moments. Some tips to cultivate this type of relationship include the following:

1. **Develop a sex-positive culture within your home.** This means that sexuality and sexual behavior are discussed in a positive, age-appropriate way. It means acknowledging that sexual development is a normal part of life and can be enjoyed when it's safe, it's consensual, and the time is right. Parents who are sex-positive do not use scare tactics, describe age-appropriate sexual activity as "bad" or "dirty," or shame others for sexual thoughts or questions.

Depending on the culture in which a parent was raised, maintaining a sex-positive atmosphere might be challenging. Some parents cringe during their first conversations with their kids about sex, because they feel awkward and unsure how their child will respond to new, potentially uncomfortable information. Other parents struggle to discuss sex as their children age and become sexual beings in their own right, especially given that the current generation of teens has had significantly more exposure to sexual content than their parents did at that age.

But it's incredibly important, and not as hard as it may seem. Parents can initiate a sex-positive home by using technically accurate terms (for example, *penis, vagina, masturbation, ejaculation,* etc.), maintaining a lighthearted tone while talking about sex, staying abreast of scientifically accurate information and resources, and regularly having brief discussions (rather than one big "talk" conducted at the age of 13 with minimal eye contact and a book with cartoon figures). Parents need to ask questions, listen as nonjudgmentally as possible, and refrain from lecturing.

And while finding a good time to bring up sexuality might seem like a challenge, it's not. It's really, really, *really* not. Sexual messages are everywhere, from TV to social media to ads, so it's easy for the mindful parent to "find a good time" to bring up sexual topics. As the parent of a passel of teens, I can tell you that their conversations are riddled with sex-adjacent references, and it's easy to casually shift the conversation to access their thoughts about a topic or revisit some essential information.

Teen: OMG, there's a picture on social media of Jada making out with Leigh!

Parent: Oh, are they dating?

Teen: No, they're just hanging out.

Parent: So hooking up but not really together?

Teen: Yeah.

Parent: Think your friends are responsible enough to practice safe sex?

Teen: I guess.

Parent: Are *you* responsible enough to practice safe sex?

Teen: Mom! You know I'm on the pill.

Parent: I do know that. But remember, the pill will keep you from getting pregnant but it doesn't protect you from sexually transmitted infections. You know, like gonorrhea or HIV.

Teen: I know, I know. That's why you need to use condoms, too.

What if your teen doesn't want to talk about sex, even during brief, casual exchanges? This can be tough, because learning this information shouldn't be optional. If you can, ask your teen what method of communication would make them comfortable. Would they rather learn about sexuality via written material? A discussion with another trusted adult? A few carefully vetted videos? Also, remind your teen that if they're too embarrassed to talk about sex with anyone, they probably shouldn't be doing it. At minimum, healthy sex requires communication with your partner as well as a health provider. On the other hand, what if your teen is a TMI kind of person and it makes you internally scream? First of all, listen closely enough to make sure that what they're saying is accurate and they're not in any unsafe situations.

Secondly, it's okay to set a boundary around the nature of your conversations. You're parent and child, not friends. So while it's essential that your teen view you as a safe person to ask questions of and to help them process emotions, being sex-positive and accessible doesn't mean you have to hear details about your teen's favorite sexual position.

2. **Educate your teens about pornography.** Curiosity about sexual behavior is normal, and that often leads to kids and teens seeking out porn. The average age of first exposure to porn is 13 years old, although nearly 50 percent of kids are first exposed to pornographic images or videos accidentally. Approximately 70 percent of teens between the ages of 15 and 17 note that they view pornography "somewhat" or "very" often, and about 70 percent of visitors to pornography websites are males.

   While there is not enough research conducted on the risks and benefits associated with pornography, professionals tend to agree that porn is extremely accessible; has the potential to replace sexual education from parents or medical professionals in a teen's mind; and can contribute to unrealistic beliefs about the role of men and women in a sexual encounter, what sex looks and feels like, and how a sexual encounter evolves. Early exposure has also been associated with negative effects, such as enduring sexist attitudes toward women.

   In order to counteract this information, parents need to speak openly about pornography. Acknowledge that it's accessible to teens and that exposure is probably inevitable, then discuss the differences between porn and real sex (it's messier and can be more awkward, not everyone has an amazing time all the time, and condoms should be present). Make sure to also keep them abreast of the current information about the impact of porn on sexual identity (I've been known to forward my teens an article or two, then bring it up again at dinner).

Parent: We've talked about pornography before, right?
Teen: Yes. Like a billion times.
Parent: I wanted to share with you something I heard. Apparently, someone at school made a sex tape with their boyfriend and it was forwarded via text. I'm wondering if you saw it.
Teen: Ugh. Yes. I know one of the people in it. I didn't forward it to anyone. I know that I'm never supposed to do that. I deleted it.
Parent: How did it make you feel to see that?

Say This, Not That!

Teens learn about sex—both accurate and inaccurate information—at a much earlier age than their parents did. Sexual terminology, innuendo, sexting, and pornography are often referred to in casual conversations today, and teens don't always have the sense that adults may be surprised or uncomfortable about their degree of sexual knowledge. In that vein, it's also important to recognize that by the time teens are in late adolescence, they may not perceive nude or sexual images or videos of themselves as embarrassing.

While I cannot think of anything more embarrassing than having a naked picture of myself on the Internet, many teens and young adults do not feel this way. To them, it may even seem inevitable, and they are not considering ramifications such as criminal charges resulting from transmitting child porn; having a work supervisor, coach, or admissions advisor see it; or even having their children encounter it one day far in the future.

A 10th grade student once told me, "Kids who have naked pictures going around are actually kind of popular. Especially if they look good in it." Here are some ways to get these possibly nerve-racking conversations started:

SAY THIS	NOT THAT
In your view, how do teens know if they're ready to be in a sexual relationship?	You're too young, so don't even think about it.
Everyone has sexual feelings.	Boys only want one thing. Girls just need to say no. Don't let them take advantage of you.
Teens are often curious about porn. You may have looked at it. Do you have any questions?	I'd better not catch you watching that filth.
It's a good idea to know as much information as possible about sex so when the time comes, you can make decisions that are right for you.	Talking about sex and birth control options is going to make you want to do it.

BIG EMOTIONS AND OVERALL MENTAL HEALTH

The fact is, adolescents are more emotionally intense than adults. Their emotions tend to be big. On a scale of 1 to 10, teens' emotions always seem to be hovering at the very low (1 to 3) or the very high (8 to 10) end, with little time spent in the moderate range. Teens are often described as "overly emotional," "moody," "unpredictable," and even "explosive." Parents report that they feel like they're "walking on eggshells," because their teen's demeanor often seems unpredictable. Teens, similarly, feel the whiplash of their moods and admit that although they can usually identify a trigger for their emotions, they often don't know how to moderate them. The combination of teens' natural quest to gain independence and the big emotions that they tend to direct toward their parents can cause parents to feel disconnected or even alienated from their teen. This can be stressful for parents, especially given that youths in their late adolescence are gearing up to graduate from high school and potentially leave the nest.

What's Up with the Big Emotions?

It's important for parents to recognize that teens' emotions are not irrational; they're intense. Most of the time, teens can identify the source of their excitement, frustration, or sorrow, even if they're not willing or able to verbalize it. When they do verbalize it, extreme language is often used, such as "I'm so embarrassed I want to die," "I'm so happy that I literally might explode," or "This is the worst I've ever felt in my entire life." The extremity of the words can be alarming, but factoring in the context of the situation, as well as the teen's personality and overall perception of support from friends or family, can help put these words in perspective. However, it's important that parents not automatically dismiss all extreme language; sometimes it may reveal that teens are feeling the impulse to self-harm or are experiencing other distressing emotions.

Remember that teens are happiest when they're with their friends. Feelings of elation are nearly always reserved for social situations, and parents are typically the victims of the irritable moments, the complaining, and the lethargy. If your teen doesn't seem to have friends or social connections, then it's important to prioritize supporting peer relationships by getting them involved in a special interest (such as music, art, or coding), exposing them to opportunities to be around other teens (for example, youth group, extracurricular activities, or volunteering), or connecting them to a counselor so they have a nonparent connection. They need to have an outlet to explore a new interest, feel heard by someone who is not their close family member, and engage in self-reflection. Even though you love them dearly, you cannot be their friend.

How to Connect with Your Teen

1. **Be present.** Given that teens have full schedules and inconsistent routines, and that even pinning them down for a family dinner can be a struggle, parents and teens run the risk of living parallel lives. For some parents, days go by in which their only communication with their teen is a flurry of texts. But that's not the way it has to be. Teens indicate that they find parents to be the most nurturing and supportive when they're present and engaged during time together in person. So set down your phone, minimize distractions, and tune in to both the content of your teen's words and the emotional undertone of them.

Parent: Hey, I'm glad to see you.

Teen: You, too.

Parent: How was your day? What was one tough thing and one great thing?

Teen: I had a hard math test. I only got 77 percent. But I was able to switch my Friday night shift at work to Sunday so I can go to the football game.

Parent: Good, I'm glad you got the schedule you want. Can I help with the math class in any way?

Teen: No, I just made a couple of stupid mistakes. I'm going to do an extra credit assignment.

Teens also report that they find time with their parent to be the least rewarding when they perceive the parent's conversation to be critical. Even if parents attempt to acknowledge successes, positive feelings can dissipate quickly when mistakes are mentioned—especially mistakes that teens perceive to be in the past. While parents can't and shouldn't avoid tackling tough issues all the time, it's important that not every conversation focus on stressful topics. Praise and encouragement deserve their own conversations, too.

2. **Focus on your teen's unique strengths.** Teens are most likely to thrive when they have parents who remain connected, give gentle feedback and support when necessary, and acknowledge and encourage teens' interests and strengths. This may consist of cheering them on during a baseball game, helping them apply for an academic scholarship, or continuing to pay for guitar lessons. Teens want to simultaneously fit in and feel unique, and having an interest or skill that makes them feel confident and appealing can help with this.

Parent: I love hearing you sing in your room.
Teen: I have an app that plays the background music.
Parent: It seems like you're really enjoying your voice lessons. I'm so excited for your end-of-semester concert.

3. **Communicate with your teen beyond the functional stuff.** While this seems like a no-brainer, it's not. In a busy family, it can be easy to focus on the routines or plethora of tasks that need to be done in a given day. Teens spend as little as 15 percent of their time with their family, and parents can feel pressured to use every minute of that time to lecture, prompt, and question. It can be difficult to take a breath, take in your teen's overall demeanor, or even make eye contact on a consistent basis. Teens want to be given space, listened to when they feel motivated to share, and encouraged even when they make a misstep.

Me: **Come down here and make eye contact with me for 15 minutes.**
My kid: **What? We just did this yesterday.**
Me: **No, it was two days ago. I want to see your face and your eyes. I don't care what we talk about. Just let me stare at you adoringly.**
My kid: **Fine. You're so weird.**

It's in these moments of connection that parents can assess their teen's overall well-being, as well as their stress level or degree of social discord, if they are experiencing any. Information and reminders can be gently imparted, but the primary purpose is to simply spend time with your teen for a few uninterrupted minutes during a busy week.

While adolescence is not the age when people are most at risk for suicidal behavior (it peaks during old age), there is an increase in depressive symptoms during adolescence, especially for girls. Depressed teens may experience persistent feelings of sadness, feelings of hopelessness, a loss of interest in activities they once enjoyed, or disruptions in sleep or concentration. Also troubling is the statistic that up to 25 percent of teens engage in nonsuicidal self-injury, usually cutting. Stress, low self-esteem, and self-hating thoughts contribute to this behavior, which can appear "contagious," because one teen in a peer group can influence the behavior of their friends.

Say This, Not That!

The vast majority of teens exit adolescence relatively unscathed and prepared to flourish as adults. This can be hard to remember, though, while you're in the thick of your child's adolescence, especially if your teen is going through a bumpy stage full of questionable choices, severe consequences, and a lot of storm and stress. Lots of teens go through these kinds of stages and sometimes require the support of a counselor. The best way to find out if counseling will help your teen or your family is to talk to a counselor directly. No matter how you end up supporting your teen, it's important to have hope. Here are some statements to consider using when your teen is struggling with big emotions:

SAY THIS	NOT THAT
How can I help?	Geez! What's up with you?
I'm going to leave you alone to calm down. When you're ready, we can talk more.	I hate being around you when you're like this.
It seems like this is really upsetting for you.	You always overreact.
When's a good time for us to go get lunch together?	You never want to spend time with me.

Limit or Let Go

How do we give teens more freedom while still offering structure and guidance through this stage of development? Here are a few ideas:

LIMIT	LET GO
Only ever communicating with you via text, not in person	Sometimes only communicating with you via text, not in person
Unsupervised time between your teen and a potential romantic partner, especially if they are not armed with accurate information about safe and consensual sex	Mixed-gender parties and social outings
Jokes, comments, and media that perpetuate body shaming, gender stereotyping, or non-consensual sex	Jokes or media about sexuality that may not be your sense of humor or perspective, but don't perpetuate harmful behaviors or stereotypes

Me: **So how's the rent coming?**

Son (pulls out a collection of crumpled bills, then slides a gift card across the table): **Maybe my process of being an adult who pays rent to his parents needs a little work.**

Chapter Five

Emerging Adulthood:
Leaving the Nest . . . Maybe
(Ages 19-ish to 25-ish)

EMERGING ADULTHOOD, THAT PORTION OF LIFE THAT spans from high school graduation through the mid 20s, is marked by exploration. Unlike the relative structure of high school, post–high school life comes with extensive choices that are greatly influenced by the specific experiences and opportunities available to individual young adults. Some young adults are college bound. Some are heading out into the world of work. Some may continue to live with their parents, and others live on campus, with roommates, or independently. Choices may be driven by financial freedoms or restrictions, cultural and familial expectations, degree of emotional support available from family and friends, and life experiences such as travel or a specific interest or skill. Emerging adults try out options in a quest to discover what might be most compatible with adult life.

Just as there are countless ways for emerging adults to begin to explore the world, there are also countless ways for parents to react to their children leaving the nest. Some parents are eager to ease away from the day-to-day parenting responsibilities, feeling confident in their child's ability to navigate the adult world and enjoying the shift away from authority figure toward something resembling a friend. Other parents feel a sense of loss, struggle to establish an identity independent from their role as a parent, or worry that their child is leaving the home without a healthy connection to family or the tools necessary to live a productive and emotionally fulfilling life. Mostly, however, parents feel a mixture of worry, sorrow, and anticipation. While it's difficult to adjust to the idea that your offspring's childhood is ending, it's exciting to see your child embrace work or education, new relationships, and novel experiences.

What's Going On? Characteristics Associated with Emerging Adulthood

PHYSICALLY

By the time adolescents become emerging adults, puberty has come to an end. Height peaks by age 20, muscles are at top capacity, and heart and lung functioning are at their best. People in this stage have likely engaged in some degree of sexual activity on a consistent basis, have likely experimented with substances such as drugs and alcohol, and are universally acknowledged to be adults.

EMOTIONALLY

The intense emotions of late adolescence still drive an emerging adult's mood and attitude toward life. However, because of their "adult" status, they tend not to have the push-pull dynamic with their parents about decision making, which results in a more harmonious relationship. However, anxiety surrounding new experiences such as going to college, finding a job, traveling, managing money, addressing sexual identity, and managing time may intensify, and young adults may not feel that their parents' support is as accessible as it once was. Like during other stages of childhood and adolescence, some young adults navigate this stage of life with positivity, productivity, and little drama, whereas others find this time to be confusing and stressful.

SOCIALLY

Transitioning into post–high school life can have a significant impact on the social life of emerging adults, especially if life circumstances limit their contact with their high school friends. Going off to college, moving to a different town, or getting a new job naturally exposes emerging adults to an entirely different group of people. Friends, work colleagues, romantic partners, and even celebrities and social media influencers may shape the identities of young adults, who are at their most open-minded stage of life. The peer group continues to be more influential than the family. Some young adults get stressed about their social life during this stage, feeling it is more difficult to establish deep and meaningful friendships than it was in high school, due to a lack of physical proximity and accessibility to other people. Emerging adults have the same need for connections as they did in late adolescence, but it may feel harder to satisfy that need. Other young adults, who may have found high school friendships to be stressful, enjoy the opportunity to start over and connect with more diverse peers.

Brain Change

During emerging adulthood, the brain continues to resemble that of a youth in late adolescence. The prefrontal cortex is not yet fully developed, so inhibiting impulses, planning, and organizing continue to be challenging for young adults. In addition, the brain's reward system is still highly active, motivating young adults to seek excitement and gravitate toward risky behavior. This "teen brain" doesn't really obtain adult levels of inhibition and emotional regulation until close to the age of 25, so emerging adults still attend more to the benefits of a particular behavior than the risks. Because legal adulthood is granted at 18 but cognitive adulthood isn't reached until 25, a lot of questionable decisions may be made during these years when supervision is minimal.

What to Expect

It's difficult to describe what to expect from the lives of emerging adults, given the variety and breadth of experiences that young adults have during this stage of life. Milestones such as going to college, moving out of a parent's home, or traveling may provide physical distance that contributes to changes in parent-child interaction. In contrast, young adults who continue to live at home or remain within close proximity of their parents may have a relationship that changes less drastically. Regardless of living circumstances, two characteristics are commonly noted by parents during this time: (1) the relationship between parent and child becomes more harmonious (especially when offspring leave the nest), because the emerging adult is afforded the freedom coveted during the high school years, and (2) the frequency and quality of communication between parent and child—typically via calls, texting, and video chat—is maintained, and often improves. Walk around any college campus and you'll witness a constant flow of communication between children and parents. Leaving the nest seems to trigger more mature behavior, as emerging adults are more likely to be in long-term romantic relationships, are less emotionally dependent on their parents, and report more overall life satisfaction.

However, despite the reduction in conflict between parent and child, there continue to be bouts of emotional upheaval, questionable decision making, and excessive reliance on the approval of peers. The larger the group of peers, the less conservative the choices. This stage of life is also strongly defined by emerging adults exploring their roles in romantic partnerships, gaining work experience, and constructing identities that will propel them toward adulthood.

ADULTING

Much of what parents can expect to see in their offspring during these years is driven by the cultural norms of that generation. In the United States, post-graduate life right now is shaped by finances: Costs associated with a college education have skyrocketed, and the likelihood of getting a job with a living wage has plummeted. Therefore, supporting oneself financially is a significant challenge, resulting in a considerable delay in "leaving the nest." Some youths leave home to attend college but return after a few months or years to conserve finances while they're working in entry-level jobs in their chosen fields. Boomeranging between living at home with parents and living independently can cause stress for both parties. For better or worse, it can be difficult to break out of the dynamic established during childhood when parents provided creature comforts and kids benefited from it.

Why Is Adulting So Hard Sometimes?

Adulting is hard, for sure. There are the big-ticket items, like work, socialization, time and money management, education, mental health, and romantic partnerships. Then there are the daily minutiae of adult life, like staying on top of your car maintenance, going to the dentist, and remembering which food your partner said they totally, absolutely detest (Was it chives or cilantro?). All these components are stressful, particularly for those youths who get overwhelmed easily, struggle with organization, or don't have a healthy support system.

Developing a "sense of future" is essential to setting the stage for a healthy adult mind-set and healthy adult behaviors. A sense of future means that a person can envision themselves existing in the future. The vision can be abstract ("I'm probably going to get married someday") or specific ("When I go to college, I'm going to study to become an engineer, get a job at a Fortune 500 company, get a dog, and buy a fixer-upper in California"). The important part is that the young adult can imagine a generally hopeful future for themselves, however loosely they define it. Emerging adults who can't imagine their lives beyond today have a difficult time setting goals, feeling connected, and experiencing a sense of self-competence.

What if your kid doesn't have a sense of future? Then look for other worrisome symptoms, such as depression, drug use, self-harming behavior, inability to maintain employment, and a lack of social connections. If any of these other symptoms are present, make sure your child has access to mental health care. The sooner they consider themselves an important part of their present and their future, the sooner they'll be invested in making decisions that lead them toward their goals.

How to Help Your Emerging Adult Start Their Adult Life

The primary way parents can support their emerging adult children is by constructing an adult-to-adult relationship. This differs significantly from the adult-to-child relationship that was appropriate during childhood and adolescence. Now that your child is a legal adult, your window to have any authority over your child's decisions is rapidly closing, even if your child is still living in your home (up to 40 percent of adult children move back in with their parents at least once after college). In order to foster the adult-to-adult relationship:

1. **Decide on a "start date."** Often, when teens graduate from high school, leave for college, or move back into their parents' home, there isn't acknowledgment

of the change in dynamics. Parents might vaguely hope that their child will demonstrate more maturity and independence, but may also be sending mixed messages to their child about what that looks like. For example, a parent may institute a curfew or demand the child attend church on Sunday, but then be perplexed when the teen doesn't clean up their dishes or do their own laundry. Instead, sit down and discuss a start date for when the emerging adult is expected to demonstrate more adultlike behaviors. During that conversation, elicit everyone's opinion about what behaviors are expected (paying rent, for example) from each adult in the house. It's okay to divide responsibilities by preference or what's logistically easiest (fair ≠ equal), but the emerging adult should have responsibilities that reflect their ability to contribute to the household. They should also get to benefit from age-appropriate freedoms. As time goes by, their responsibilities may change or expand as they increase adult practice and gain competence.

Parent: **What's the start date for post-graduation life? Would you prefer it to be July 1, the first full month after graduation, or September 15, your 22nd birthday?**
Emerging adult: **What's going to change after that date?**
Parent: **Let's decide together. Dad and I are thinking that you would start by paying $250 in rent per month, working a full 40 hours per week, doing all your own laundry, and mowing the lawn every other week.**
Emerging adult: **I'm okay with that. I'd also like to not have a curfew, schedule my work shifts whenever I want as long as my boss agrees, and keep the**

door to my bedroom closed so I can be messy without upsetting anyone.

2. **Focus on what you can control.** You can't control whether your young adult is on time to work, eats a healthy dinner, or pays the rent on time. But you can control whether your tone when they call is lecturing and dismissive or warm and welcoming. You can control whether you offer to help them with adulting tasks like choosing a health care plan or negotiating a lease. And you can decide how to respond if they get in a jam, such as misusing a credit card and not having enough money to make a car payment, getting arrested for trespassing while at a concert with a friend, or failing a college class. If these decisions are made with a co-parent, it's best to try to create a plan "just in case" rather than waiting until a misstep occurs and being forced to make a decision hastily.

Parent: I know you got your own car insurance policy a few weeks ago. I'm really happy about that, and really appreciate that you took the initiative on that. If you ever have any questions about how policies and all that stuff works, I'm happy to help.
Emerging adult: Okay, thanks. I think you answered all my questions when we talked about it before.
Parent: I figure we should also talk about what would happen if you ever can't use your car for some reason.
Emerging adult: What do you mean?
Parent: Well, for instance, if your car is in the repair shop and you can't drive it for a while, Mom and I are both working, so we won't be able to lend you our cars or drive you to work.
Emerging adult: I could use a ride-share service. Or get a ride from a coworker.

Parent: Those are good ideas. And I also want you to know that if something happens while you're out on the road, like a flat tire or a breakdown, you can call us to help. You're not alone in this. But we really want you to plan ahead, so if your car is out of commission for a while, you'll know what to do and won't feel panicked or overwhelmed.

Say This, Not That!

Adjusting to the change in the adult-child relationship is difficult for both parent and child. Ideally, parents will have made a slow shift to more adultlike communication as their adolescent approached graduation, but sometimes this isn't the case. In order for your emerging adult to act like an adult, they need to be treated like one. This means treating them respectfully and expecting them to follow through with their age-appropriate responsibilities. Most importantly, however, it means remembering that your role is now that of a support system rather than an authority figure. Power struggles should diminish, communication should remain open, and both parent and child should work to define the new relationship. It may be bumpy, but mutual respect should smooth the way.

Here are some suggestions for how to avoid falling back into old parent-adolescent dynamics:

SAY THIS	NOT THAT
I'd like to find a time to talk about how we can better share responsibilities in this house.	My house, my rules. Find a new place to live if you're not going to follow the rules.
We're in different phases of life right now, so I understand that your priorities are different than mine.	You are so immature.
Do you have a plan to deal with this? Do you need help making one?	You need to ... you must ... you have to ...
Let's step away from this problem and just go do something fun. We can come back to it later.	You're driving me crazy with your laziness and immaturity.
Our time together shouldn't only consist of talking about adulting. Do you have time this week to get some lunch or catch a movie?	(insert nagging)

DEVELOPING AN IDENTITY

As late adolescence transitions into emerging adulthood, there comes an intense need to establish an identity. Young adults try to make sense of their world in terms of how they fit into it. Older adolescents are shifting from viewing themselves as the center of a world that revolves around them to understanding they are part of a "we." This realization comes with a lot of pressure and confusion as to what their role should be as they enter adult life. What defines me? Where do I belong? What is my purpose? What kind of adult do I want to be? And sometimes identity development takes a sharp left turn from what they assume their parents prefer, and this can exacerbate feelings of alienation or uncertainty. Emerging adulthood is a crucial time for identity development, and exploration is key.

James Marcia, a clinical and developmental psychologist, articulated the journey that a young adult may take in their quest to develop an identity. First, it's important to recognize that identity does not consist solely of one variable, such as gender. Our identity may be composed of several domains, encompassing categories or spectrums such as gender, age, sexuality, and career exploration, as well as spiritual, parental, spousal, class, racial, or cultural identity. Although identity can and will alter throughout the life span, young adults are initiating the process of defining themselves in the context of their adult selves. While one young adult may identify as a black, male, gay artist, another may identify as a nonbinary athlete and student.

Why Is Developing an Identity So Important?

Developing an identity is essential to satisfying the emerging adult's desire to both explore and commit. The most well-adjusted young adults have had the opportunity to do both, and explore a variety of options to test whether those options reflect their values and sense of self. Only after having suitable time to explore is a young adult ready to commit to a particular path. For example, an emerging adult exploring career options may attend college, work at several internships and part-time jobs, or conduct research under the supervision of a professor. They may graduate and take any entry-level position offered, gaining experience, noting interests, strengths, and challenges. They may switch roles, get additional training, or start a completely different job. Several years after the start of working life, they may have a clearer idea of their professional purpose and commit to a chosen field or a worthy employer. Because they've had time to explore their career options extensively, their commitment feels satisfying.

When emerging adults commit to a path before they've had a chance to explore, dissatisfaction is more likely. This is most likely to occur when they've adopted an identity endorsed by an authority figure, rather than one they've come to on their own. In contrast, if they explore extensively but never feel compelled to commit (for example, go from job to job haphazardly), they might feel anxiety and a lack of purpose.

How to Help Your Emerging Adult Feel Supported as They Explore Their Identity

1. **Encourage your emerging adult to explore.** This may require biting your tongue, because the temptation to prompt your offspring to fast-forward to grown-up thinking may be strong. But as long as your child is grounded in reality enough to take care of their basic needs and remain physically and mentally healthy, they're going to benefit from trying new things, even if those things feel uncomfortable for you or contradict the values that you tried to impart during their adolescence.

   Parent: **What's your plan for this summer now that you've graduated from college?**
   Emerging adult: **I found a cool job working at the fish shop at the beach.**
   Parent: **Interesting. Were you thinking of working in computer design at all? I know how hard you worked to get your degree.**

Emerging adult: Eventually. But I think I'd like to live at the beach and have a low-stress job for a few months. Mike says he and I can share a little cottage about five miles from the beach. He's going to work there, too.

Parent: You know, I bet you'll get to try a lot of different kinds of seafood.

2. **Accept their choices.** One of the best aspects of choices is that even if they turn out to be misguided, they can almost always be modified. Your child decides to forego college in favor of starting a band? Fine. Set a boundary that the band is not going to practice at your house and determine if you're going to contribute a single dollar toward their endeavor. But lecturing, attempting to change their mind, or criticizing their rationale is likely going to cause your child to disconnect from you and classify you as unsupportive.

Emerging adult: I've decided that I'm going to hold off on taking college classes this fall.

Parent: Really? What's your plan instead of college?

Emerging adult: Sybil, Mark, Jake, and I are going to see if we can get our band some gigs.

Parent: Interesting. I really don't know anything about how one would do that. What would you do for money? Would you need to travel?

Emerging adult: Well, I have some money from graduation, but we're also going to work jobs during the week. On the weekend, we're going to travel to bars and clubs to perform. Mark has a big SUV we can use. We're all going to chip in for gas and repairs.

Parent: You sound excited.

3. **Recognize that acceptance isn't the same as endorsement.** You can accept your emerging adult's choices without encouraging them or sending a message of agreement. Ideally, your child will be mature enough to handle hearing that they're making a decision that differs from your preferences. But they may be particularly sensitive to your feedback, and may default to assuming that you're being unsupportive. It will be important to express a difference of opinion in a calm manner.

Parent: I can tell you're excited about working at the beach for the summer.
Emerging adult: Yeah, definitely.
Parent: I have to admit, I do wish you were looking for jobs in computer design. You worked hard and you're really talented. Plus, you have some student loans to pay off.
Emerging adult: I know. I *will*. But I don't want to get a grown-up job just yet. I want to hang at the beach with Mike. I don't want you to keep bugging me about this.
Parent: No, I've said my piece. I wanted to tell you how I feel, but I understand that you've made a choice about how you're going to spend your summer. I really do hope it's a positive experience for you.

Say This, Not That!

Forming an identity is one of the most crucial aspects of transitioning into adult life, and it's essential that parents give their child the freedom to undergo this process, even if it's confusing ("I'm completely supportive of her being gay, but she's so immersed in gay culture that she doesn't socialize with any of her old friends . . . she dresses differently and hasn't been to church with our family in six months . . . is this a phase or is this how she'll be for the remainder of her adult life?"). Emerging adults will make their own choices, and it's important that they have the room to experience them fully; if they encounter negative consequences, they can more mindfully steer themselves toward positive choices. Some parents report feeling as though their adult child rejected aspects of their childhood that they themselves felt proud of, and there can be associated feelings of grief.

Remember, your child is going to go through many transitions throughout their life, and if you remain a firm supporter, you'll get to grow and change with your child. Here are some ways to let them know that you're now here to support them rather than act as an authority figure:

SAY THIS	NOT THAT
I'm here to help.	You should . . .
Mistakes are important. They help you learn what to do and what not to do.	You're old enough to know better.
I'm not sure I understand your thinking. Can you explain it to me in more detail?	This is a bad idea.
Your choices are not what I would have predicted, and I'm struggling to accept them. I definitely need more time to adjust.	We didn't raise you to act this way.
You're an adult and that means you get to make your own choices.	I want you to learn from my mistakes. So listen to what I'm saying . . .

How to Let Go and Worry Less

Develop a mantra. Seriously. Although you may feel in control of your anxiety about your young adult's choices most of the time, there are moments that can feel overwhelming. During these times, consider doing the following: (1) close your eyes; (2) take several deep breaths, making sure to breathe in through your nose and out through your mouth; and (3) repeat the words "My child is now an adult. I taught them well. They are smart, capable, and loved. They will learn from their mistakes and will flourish." Write this mantra on a piece of paper, post it in your line of sight, and distract yourself with another activity until the worst of your fretting has passed.

References

American Psychological Association. https://www.apa.org/monitor/2016/03/puberty.

American Psychological Association. https://www.apa.org/news/press/releases/2017/08/pornography-exposure.

Belsky, J. (2018). *Experiencing Childhood and Adolescence.* Worth Publishers, New York.

Caron, S.L. & Moskey, E.G. (2002). Changes over time in teenage sexual relationships: Comparing the high school class of 1950, 1975, and 2000. *Adolescence, 37,* 515–526.

Finer, L.B. & Philbin, J.M. (2014). Trends in ages at key reproductive transitions in the United States, 1951–2010. *Women's Health Issues* 24 (3), 1–9.

Influence Central. http://influence-central.com/kids-tech-the-evolution-of-todays-digital-natives.

Lawler, M., & Nixon E. (2011). Body dissatisfaction among adolescent boys and girls: The effects of body mass, peer appearance, culture and internalization of appearance ideals. *Journal of Youth and Adolescence, 40,* 59–71.

Merikangas, K.R., He J.P., Burstein, M., et al (2010). Lifetime prevalence of mental disorders in US adolescents: Results from the national comorbidity survey replication-adolescent supplement (NCS-A). *Journal of the American Academy of Child and Adolescent Psychiatry, 49,* 980–989.

UNFPA (2015). *Emerging evidence, lessons, and practice in comprehensive sexuality education, a global review.* Paris, France: UNESCO.

Resources

Chapman, Gary. *The 5 Love Languages of Teenagers: The Secret to Loving Teens Effectively.* Chicago: Northfield Publishing, 2016.

Child Development Institute. https://childdevelopmentinfo.com.

Child Mind Institute. www.childmind.org.

Common Sense Media. www.commonsensemedia.org.

Lahey, Jessica. *The Gift of Failure: How the Best Parents Learn to Let Go So Their Children Can Succeed.* New York: Harper, 2016.

Marcia, James. "Identity in Adolescence," in *Handbook of Adolescent Psychology*, edited by Richard M. Lerner and Laurence Steinberg. New York: Wiley & Sons, 1980.

Price, Adam. *He's Not Lazy: Empowering Your Son to Believe in Himself.* New York: Sterling, 2017.

Siegel, Daniel. *Brainstorm: The Power and Purpose of the Teenage Brain.* New York: Penguin, 2014.

Index

A

Active noncompliance, 29
Adolescence
  defined, 2–5
  stages of, 5–6
Adulting, 110–115
Anxiety, 31–38
Avoidance, 31–38

B

Body acceptance, 90
Boundaries
  developing, 82–88
  resistance to, 23–31
Brain development, 6–8
  emerging adulthood, 108
  late adolescence, 73
  middle adolescence, 44

C

Comparison, 51–56
Consent, 86–87
Control, 48–49

D

Decision-making, 80–81
Depression, 101
Dishonesty, 16–22
Disrespect, 26–29

E

Early adolescence, 5, 11–13
  anxiety and
    avoidance, 31–38
  dishonesty, 16–22
  emotional characteristics
    of, 14
  limit or let go, 39
  physical characteristics
    of, 13
  social characteristics of, 14
  testing limits, 23–31
  what to expect, 16
Emerging adulthood, 6,
    105–106
  adulting, 110–115
  emotional characteristics
    of, 107
  identity development,
    115–120
  physical characteristics
    of, 106
  social characteristics of,
    107–108
  what to expect, 109
Emotions. *See* Feelings and
  emotions
Empathy, 54
Experimentation, 74–81

F

Failure, 37
Feelings and emotions
    early adolescence, 14
    emerging adulthood,
        107–108
    late adolescence, 72, 96–102
    middle adolescence, 43
    parental, 8–9
Friendships, 45–51, 76–77, 98

H

Hyperrationality, 76, 80

I

Identity development, 115–120
Impulse control, 46
Intuition, 80–81
Irrational thinking, 53–54

L

Late adolescence, 5–6, 69–70
    boundary
        development, 82–88
    emotional characteristics
        of, 72
    emotions and mental
        health, 96–102
    limit or let go, 103
    physical characteristics
        of, 71–72
    risky behavior, 74–81
    sex and romantic
        partnerships, 88–96
    social characteristics
        of, 72–73
    what to expect, 74

Limits, testing, 23–31
Lying, 16–22

M

Mantras, 121
Marcia, James, 116
Mental health, 96–102
Middle adolescence, 5, 41–42
    emotional characteristics
        of, 43
    friendships and social
        pressure, 45–51
    limit or let go, 67
    physical characteristics
        of, 42–43
    skill development and
        responsibilities, 61–66
    social characteristics
        of, 43
    social comparison, 51–56
    technology and social
        media, 56–61
    what to expect, 44–45

N

Negotiation, 25–26
Neuroplasticity, 7
"No," saying, 29
Noncompliance, 29–30

P

Passive noncompliance, 29
Peer pressure, 45–51, 76–77
Perceptions, 33
Pornography, 94–95
"Practice the no," 29
Problem-solving, 37–38

Puberty, 2–5
    early, 15
    middle adolescence, 42–43
    parental response to, 12

R

Relational aggression, 46
Responsibilities, 61–66
Risky behavior, 74–81
Romantic partnerships, 88–96
Rules, resistance to, 23–31

S

Safety, and setting
    boundaries, 82–83
Self-esteem, 14, 34, 52, 90
Self-injury, 101
Self-reflection, 78–79
Self-talk, 54–56

Sense of future, 110–111
Sex and sexuality,
    71–72, 88–96
Sex hormones, 44
Siegel, Daniel, 76
Skill development, 61–66
Social comparison, 51–56
Social media, 3–4, 56–61
Social pressure, 45–51, 76–77
Suicidal behavior, 101

T

Technology, 56–61
Temperament, 12

V

Verbal abuse, 31
Verbal disrespect, 26–29

About the Author

 **Tara Egan, D.Ed.**, founder of Charlotte Parent Coaching, LLC (www.charlotteparent coaching.com), has nearly 20 years of experience as a school psychologist, parent coach, counselor, public speaker, and adjunct professor. She specializes in working with parents of children and teens with social, emotional, and behavioral issues. She is the author of *Better Behavior for Ages 2–10: Small Miracles That Work Like Magic* and provides training to school professionals, parents, and other mental health clinicians on topics such as best practices in parenting, social media usage in children and teens, and behavioral management in school and in the home environment. Dr. Egan is the mother of two and the stepmother of four. Every day her children remind her that of all her job responsibilities, being a parent is her most important role.

CPSIA information can be obtained
at www.ICGtesting.com
Printed in the USA
LVHW051933220120
644449LV00026B/589